C0-BEG-667

*Common Sense Credit*

# *COMMON*

## CREDIT UNIONS COME OF AGE

*The Devin-Adair Company   New York, 1962*

# SENSE CREDIT

*Charles Morrow Wilson*

*Canadian agent: Thomas Nelson & Sons Ltd., Toronto*
*Library of Congress catalog card number: 62–20037*

*Manufactured in the United States of America,*
*by H. Wolff, New York*
*Designed by Robin Fox*

# *Foreword*

The Canadian Alphonse Desjardins, a founder of the credit union movement, said: "The credit union . . . is the expression in the field of economics of a high social ideal."

In this book, Charles Morrow Wilson tells, in his own common sense style and in the simple, yet eloquent, words of people who belong to credit unions, today's story of Desjardins' expression in action. From the shops and factories of U. S. industry, from the plains of the Texas Panhandle, and from the parishes and fishing banks of Canada —from everywhere in North America—Mr. Wilson has gathered the anecdotes and the spirit of today's credit unions.

Mr. Wilson has also recreated, in warm and human fashion, the personal adventure story, the devotion and the dedication of Roy F. Bergengren, whose crusade during the years between 1921 and 1945 did so much to bring the credit union to millions of Americans.

Finally "Common Sense Credit" tells how credit unions

are keeping up with a changing world, and how the credit union philosophy of self-help and self-determination is being carried to the people of the emerging countries of the free world.

Charles Morrow Wilson traveled the length and breadth of North America to find the subjects who fill the pages of his book. They are people of all kinds, of all races, creeds and religions; but people who hold a common belief in the credit union idea of self-help. If there is such a thing as "ordinary" people, the people of this book are that kind of people. But they are people who have built for themselves and for each other an extraordinary kind of financial institution; and, from his wealth of writing experience and innate understanding of people, Mr. Wilson has written an extraordinary book.

"Common Sense Credit" is extraordinary in the sense that it is more than a book about credit, more than a book about people, and more than a book about an idea. It is a book dedicated in a matter-of-fact manner to the dignity of free men and women, to the homespun humor of the self-reliant breed, and, to the integrity of the common man. It is a book about the past, the present and the future of credit unions and the people they serve; but above all, a book that is unique because human beings are, as individuals, unique.

Credit unions are based upon a "common bond" concept, upon the principle that people are more important than money, and upon the idea that the best way to help oneself is to help one's brother. There are those who ridicule this concept, who profess to believe that those who run credit unions are just as selfishly motivated as are those who run loan companies or banks. This may, in a sense, be true; but only in a limited sense. For most of those who run credit unions are volunteers, who ask for and receive no pay, and who feel a missionary zeal for their work not generally found in any institution outside the church—a zeal which sometimes mystifies and perplexes those who consider credit unions their competitors in the field of personal finance.

Perhaps, one must be a credit union worker, or at least a credit union member, to fully appreciate the words of Desjardins linking the credit union to both economics and "a high social ideal." But anyone who reads this book of Charles Morrow Wilson's cannot help but appreciate Desjardins' words.

For Charles Morrow Wilson has chronicled in this book not only the deeds, but the temper, the disposition and the spirit of the people of the credit union movement. "Common Sense Credit" makes not only common sense, but extraordinarily good sense—and extraordinarily good reading.

R. C. MORGAN
*President,*
*Credit Union National Association*
*June, 1962*

# *Contents*

*Common Sense Credit*

[ 1

# *Credit Unions—Everlasting Amateurs*

A credit union is a group of people who join in saving money individually, pooling the savings as a group enterprise, so that all members of the group may benefit from borrowing and lending at moderate interest rates. A credit union is a legally chartered nonprofit corporation, run by amateurs.

"Amateur" is an engaging word. By usual dictionary definition an amateur is a "lover of any art, sport, game or cause who does not practice it for gain only." In our living language an amateur is an individual with interests and devotion who applies them to a given endeavor without seeking or receiving money as a prime objective or a goal directly sought. The amateur is not necessarily a beginner, but he remains a learner. Even the greatest champions frequently elect to remain amateurs.

The credit union movement is remarkably well endowed with leaders, directors and other worker members who keep the status of amateurs as regards the work they do for credit unions. Only a minority of credit unions pay any of their workers in salaries, or wages. Practically all elected officers, directors, and committee members including those of the key committees—supervisory, credit and educational—serve without monetary pay. In the United States alone about a third of a million men and women serve credit unions for love instead of money. In no other financial institution do so many actively serve a cause, an economic utility or a democratic fundamental with such devoted amateurism.

By overwhelming majority the everlasting learners of the credit union movement remain the everlasting amateurs thereof. Even the small proportion who presently turn professional almost invariably begin as amateurs. This bears importantly on the credit union character, learning processes, and total development.

These, of course, are very general summaries. By contrast a credit union's work is enormously specific, unendingly detailed, and necessarily molded to the changing views and needs of the particular people who are the credit union. One sees the proof most impressively in such a place as the Greater Chicago area, where more than 800 credit unions, nine-tenths of them industrial, are now flourishing. The loop city, which is so essentially anybody's hometown, has quietly taken its place as one of the major arenas of the American credit union.

For a typical and fairly definitive story, take the Dreis Krump Credit Union in Southside Chicago.

Dreis and Krump is a medium-sized metalworks, which employs about 500 skilled or semiskilled metal and machine tool workers, all labor union members. The firm manufactures sheet metal fabrication machinery. Until 1953 the organization had no credit facility in or near the plant. Workers who direly needed money were accustomed to borrowing from the big boss, Walter Dreis, the company's president. The boss in turn was accustomed to thinning his wallet by making advances ranging from $10 to $100 which he figuratively wrote on his cuffs. Quite frequently the cuff writings were permanently lost the instant the boss's shirt went to the laundry. Some of the touch loans were repaid. An indefinite number, quite possibly a majority, vanished down the laundry chute. Walter Dreis happens to be a kindly, creative man who likes both people and machines more than he likes money, and sees money merely as a means for helping people and machines.

But the boss's personal wallet could not begin to fulfill the credit needs of some half a thousand family heads. Too many of his employees, including an actual majority of the newcomers, became intermittent or continuous victims of loan sharks and installment salesmen. As a result wages were attached, bill collectors invaded working floors, good employees showed conspicuous evidence of too much worrying and the wrong kind of eating.

The first move to remedy took the form of employee aid funds, known informally as department "kitties." Employees who wished to take part contributed a dollar a month from wages to their department fund. They elected a treasurer, or "kitty keeper," who served without pay and handed out money where and to whom it was most needed. The aid funds were mostly directed to unpredictable needs and acts of God or fate, and such items as medical care not otherwise available, and for tragic or urgent needs in the homes of members. The aid funds were all to the good; there just weren't enough of them.

Early in October, 1953, about 45 employees assembled to discuss and apply for a credit union charter. The moving spirits demonstrated they were also bold spirits. At first the boss did not approve and many of the employees thought that a credit union was some kind of an adjunct to a labor union.

But from the beginning the founders saw their proposed credit union as a brotherly enterprise. It would have to serve all in a democratic manner. It could be subservient to no cliques or factions. Of the first twelve directors, nine were from the shop and three were from management. But all pledged themselves to the service of the credit union. The boss heeded this, presently withdrew his personal objections and gave his unreserved blessings to the fledgling credit union, granted it the only available niche of office space, then asked the moving spirits to let him know what else he could do for "the cause." They thanked him and said, "Nothing else!"

Perhaps appropriately the first meeting place of the original forty members and the original office space for the Dreis and Krump Employees Credit Union was the shop's cell-sized first aid room. There Jack Rogers, a die-setter who was voted the first unpaid treasurer, set up shop. The original credit committee also met in the tiny, one-desk, two-chair room and, as needs required, the twelve directors and the three members of the supervisory committee also crowded in. Thirty charter members showed at the first meeting; about fifty at the second. The rest of the potential membership waited to see what would happen. Their usual question was, "Why do I need a credit union?" Jack Rogers, Bill Boyle and the rest of the charter members undertook to explain what credit unions are for.

The explanations were progressively effective. Within a month the active membership grew to about 70, within six months to 377, within six years to 555, considerably more than the total roster of employees. Spouses and children of employees are eligible for membership, as they have been since the beginning.

The rapid upgrowth of membership left the unpaid treasurer and his assistants holding a large and fast growing bear by its short tail. They couldn't turn loose and they had no desire to. Jack Rogers qualified himself as a capable treasurer by completing an adult-education night course in bookkeeping. With the help of about a dozen member volunteers among fellow employees, he devoted as many as four or five nights per week and Saturday afternoons to keeping up with the multiplying work. On a great many Sundays, after church, Rogers and his wife and their young daughter would settle themselves about the dining room table and spend most of the afternoon and early evenings balancing the passbooks, and posting the weekend ledgers. They worked with the comforting assurance that when additional help was needed, it was as near as the telephone and as free as the Chicago breeze. "At first," the charter treasurer and long time president reflects, "it was a matter of the blind leading the blind. Then all at once all of us began to see."

The first year proved to be one of determined share growth and torrential loan applications. Contrary to predictions by a few skeptics, the credit needs of members proved to be demanding and oftentimes emotional. The amateur treasurer doubled as personal counselor. One of the first confiders was a man who was certain that suicide was the only solution to his financial problems. Having first pointed out that departed spirits are no great shakes at welding steel or otherwise earning wages, Rogers enrolled the despondent worker as a credit union member and the credit committee outlined and arranged a substantial loan, plus an approved program of savings whereby shares as well as loan repayments were deducted from the employee's earnings. Another advice seeker confided that the only way he could ever save money was to divorce his wife. Rogers suggested to the member that he was too homely to count on getting another wife; then he and the credit committee worked out another loan-and-shares buying program which presently saw the member not only out of debt but more comfortably placed in matrimony.

Home improvements, income tax payment, and consolidation of debts were and remain the predominant credit needs. Despite the relatively enlightened anti-usury laws of Illinois the need for protection against loan sharks soon became as obvious as a country washday and at least as revealing.

Employee after employee called at the undersized office to explain desperate needs for relief from installment payments and from fine-print sales contracts which leave wage earners paying interest of well above 14 per cent and facing chattel mortgages or nagging demands related to just about everything they "almost" owned, from the clothes on their backs to the beds they slept in. The continuing saga of credit needs included employees who were in debt for phony jewelry, overpriced watches, used autos which were altogether too much used, and a thousand other overpriced belongings with a long list of payments due. A loyal old-timer confided that he was loaded down with chattel debts totaling more than $4,700. Treasurer Rogers and the credit committee figured out a combination savings and debt bunching program whereby the old-timer gradually erased his indebtedness at a steady rate of $95 a month.

As the first frantic rush for loans abated, the treasurer and credit committee with the blessings of the directors developed their methods for facing up to the increasing applications for supplemental loans. They avoid absolute rules. They accept the credit union's practice of considering each loan application completely on its own merits. They also keep the working gospel of making every borrower a shareholder, stressing the vital correlation of borrowing and saving.

Though the average loan stays between $600 and $700, the proportion of loans in excess of $1,000 grows steadily. From the first there has been continuing demand for what many bankers term "appendage loans." Joe Jones, for example, borrows $800 to reroof his home. The completed job comes to about $900. Joe hurries to the credit union to apply for an additional loan of $100. The credit union usually grants the "additional". But the treasurer shows Joe his share account and says gently, "No more upping of your loans without upping your shares."

Today the treasurer and the credit committee make even greater use of the mail and telephone. Nowadays sick members have only to mail or phone in their applications and, as needs require, loan checks are delivered at their homes or hospitals the following day. When members transfer to other plants or move on to other jobs, the Dreis-Krump Credit Union invites them to retain membership and conduct their usual business with stamped, addressed envelopes furnished by the union, especially if a credit union is not available in the new situation. From first introduction the mail enterprise has worked like a charm. It is now extended to wives and children of plant workers and to sales personnel and others not headquartered at the home plant. To better serve the home folks the credit union has expanded office hours from the original one per workday (11:30 A.M. to 12:30 P.M.) to include an afternoon hour for the benefit of night shift workers.

As the credit union continued to win acceptance, loan applications began assuming personalized urgency. For example, Louis Ketch, a revered old-timer, was stricken with spinal cancer. He phoned in for an emergency loan of $500 to pay tabs for all the necessary treatments. The credit committee joined together in a special lunch hour meeting and within the hour the unpaid treasurer was at the stricken member's home delivering the cash.

Another charter member became a victim of a serious auto wreck. His loan collateral was instantly changed to crumpled worthlessness and his company-provided accident insurance was of no avail. A double-time loan from the credit union tided over the victim's family. Within six weeks the injured man was duly mended, back at work and recipient of a renewed loan for a renewed auto, which has outlasted the loan's repayment by a good three years.

J. W., a shopman with 17 years seniority, didn't take to credit unions at first. After a year of "waiting around to see how it works out" J. W. presently joined and authorized a payroll deduction of $10 monthly for purchasing shares. This turned out to be the buy of a lifetime. Previously J. W., though one of the plant's best workers, had been by his own admission one of the world's worst money handlers. "I lack sales resistance," J. W. confided. It was an engagingly honest statement but it was being made by telephone and from a nearby jail.

Month after month, year after year, J. W. had been taking the lure of installment buying. Accordingly he owed by the week for his Sunday suit, his apartment furnishings, his wife's jewelry, his watch, overcoat, auto, and a varied array of accessories. For years he had worked on through a perennial assortment of bill collectors and a thickening haze of chattel mortgages. Then, all at a turn, a flying wedge of bill collectors clipped him from behind. The total onrush included the state income tax department and the U.S. Internal Revenue Service. Both of the latter reiterated that J. W. had failed to fill out the required forms on his non-salary income. It was a long story—too long to explain from the jail house telephone.

So the credit union went to work. First an emergency loan got the member out of jail. A show-all-cards visit with the credit committee produced a four-digit "debt-integration" loan with payroll security. J. W. used the loan to pay income taxes and penalties, and to repay all outstanding debts. After 19 months this financially transformed member was squared away with the credit union. Nowadays when fast talking salesmen close in on him, J. W. tells them he will discuss their fascinating offers with the treasurer of his credit union.

Bill Boyle, erstwhile steel welder who is now the manager, points out that Dreis-Krump isn't a big credit union and doesn't aspire to be. Even so, its first six years of operation built up assets of $304,644, and it's still growing.

From its beginning the credit union has rebated five per cent of interest charges. During its first two years dividend earnings were two per cent; since then they have been four per cent. But the unsalaried directors and officers and the membership agree that neither bigness of assets nor fatness of dividends is their goal.

Rather the common goal was and is effective integration of service to all members, agreeable and democratic relationships between members and officers, independent integrity of the credit union as such and, of course, solvency and survival. Strikes are the hard test of this composite goal. Though the shop union (International Association of Machinists) and the Dreis and Krump management are both distinctly above average in what politicians and college professors sometimes term social consciousness, strikes still occur.

When a strike "hits", the credit union automatically limits the loans to $200 (except under very special circumstances), opens the cash drawer, and waits it out.

By mutual consent the credit union stays open for business in its assigned office space within the shop, and the credit committee remains on call. For the duration of the strike, collections are on a pay-if-you-can, otherwise-don't-worry basis. Though the latter predominates after the first month of strike, a majority of member-borrowers keep their interest paid and some members keep right on paying their loans and investing in shares. "It's impossible," Bill Boyle avows, "but it keeps right on happening, because more and more of our members regard this credit union like a wife or husband—taken for better or worse. . . ."

Between file straightening and posting books Bill Boyle murmurs: "This here is a pretty good credit union. It takes root in a good industry and a good shop. It's for all our people and taken by all; our people are good folks, a fine, hard working, law-abiding, God-fearing family."

With variations, one encounters this sentiment wherever one talks and lives credit unions, including the International Harvester Company's credit unions. The great McCormick organization has a whole string of credit unions: there are thirteen in the Central Area (Chicago to Memphis) alone. One of them is to be found in the McCormick Melrose Park plant, immediately outside Chicago.

This establishment employs more than 2,000 workers; of these approximately 1,000 are Negroes and about 60 are Oriental or other Americans of color. The integration is magnificent; skin color has no association with the credit union's administration of credit.

Melrose Park Credit Union began in 1949. Its first year closed with about 150 members with shareholdings totaling about $10,000. The present membership, including spouses and children of workers, is about 2,500 (potential plus 500); assets of around $525,000 and growing. The woman treasurer is paid half time. All other services are contributed by amateurs.

The current average loan is about $650 and steadily rising. Up to half of all loans are directed to home furnishing and improvements, i.e., repairs, reroofing, storm windows, and building additional bedrooms, etc. Christmas loans, back-to-school loans and setting-up-housekeeping loans and vacation loans are frequent. Home appliances, children's medical and dental expenses, tuition and other school investments are among the more rapidly increasing reasons for borrowing.

The recurring and sometimes crucial problem is that of tiding through the seasonal layoffs and/or the intermittent "drags" of underpar employment. The plant workers who lead, direct and are the credit union understand the human and expedient art of helping their borrowers pull through. They do not lose loans, but in many instances they "re-issue the paper" and extend payment time, depending on ever-changing needs, from a few days to as much as five years. The credit union meticulously avoids pressure techniques for collecting, rarely resorts to wage assignments, but makes a virtual fetish of collecting interest even during periods of strikes or layoffs.

The layoff hazards have atoning factors. International Harvester wages are consistently above national averages. And at least as of this date, about 95 per cent of layoff victims are in due time taken back on payroll. The prevailing "sub-benefits" which include two-thirds of base pay for the first 26 weeks of unemployment usually cushion financial shocks and facilitate regular interest payments as well as methodical purchase of shares. Voluntary payroll deductions, normally ranging from $29,000 to $35,000 weekly, are more frequently for share purchases than loan repayment, and serve to minimize the need for co-signers; also to keep share ownership the most used collateral. Al Shaff, a charter member and the long-time president, summarizes: "We don't set the world afire here. We don't try to. But we keep a family style credit union which is as sound as our industry . . . which we believe is about all any bunch of amateurs can expect to do."

In a big city like Chicago, visiting credit unions will take you to hundreds of places—from marble foyers to tar paper shacks, from railroad sentry boxes to riverboat docks, from the stockyards to City Hall. In one case, at least, it will take you backstage in a rehearsal hall.

For a credit union with a flavorful difference, consider the Musichorale Credit Union. This is a tiny credit union of barely 100 members, but from the standpoint of novelty and pure charm its story will match any other you can trace through the records of the credit union movement. It serves a singing society called Musichorale, Inc., a non-sponsored and self-powered choral group which came into existence back in 1946. The 75 singing members of Musichorale bill themselves as "Chicagoland's Busiest Singers," and they are probably right. Not only do they rehearse every Tuesday evening—no excuses allowed—but they also fill up to three additional musical engagements a month, booked at nominal fees by churches and business firms, civic organizations and charities. The income from these performances, augmented by an annual fund-raising concert, has enabled the Musichorale members to establish a firm economic foundation for their harmonizing. They have been able to purchase their own robes and music, and, incredibly, to buy their own rehearsal building on 59th Street near Kedzie, in a residential section of southwest Chicago not far from Midway Airport. Meanwhile they have developed themselves into a technically superb chorus, with a wide repertoire and rich experience in every type of choral work from show tunes to sacred music. All this keeps them busy.

The purpose of Musichorale, Inc., is simply to sing. The original group was a chorus formed at Lindbloom High School in southeast Chicago, whose members decided in 1946 to maintain their group after graduation. Some of these people still remain, including the director, a remarkably endowed musician named Arthur Silhan, who once sang with the Lyric Opera Company and has since taught music in the civic school system; his wife is the capable accompanist and arranger for the chorus. Those singers who have dropped out have been replaced from the waiting list by other singers, ranging from middle-aged married couples to teen-agers, but all are selected after comprehensive auditions by the music committee. Youngsters have to prove, by showing their report cards, that they are maintaining good grades in school, or be dropped from the chorus. Some of these dedicated people come many miles to perform with the group, not only from remote sections of Chicago, but also from downstate Illinois and Indiana. Every member pays annual dues of $15 for the privilege of belonging. As one admirer said, "They sure like singing, to work so hard at it."

They also like helping people. Besides the busy singing schedule already described, the chorus stages two benefit concerts each year, donating the money to a handicapped children's fund espoused by the society. They have started a regular blood donorship program within their group. They contribute appearances at hospitals and old peoples' homes. Musichorale gives as part of its stated purpose a determination to be "a force in the community for personal integrity and social responsibility." Recently a second chorus was organized for children, called the Musichorale Miniature, also numbering 75 voices. These children receive an enviable musical training, emerging as accomplished choristers at age 16. They also learn the kind of socially responsible habits so happily exemplified by the adult chorus.

Among such inspired amateurs, the credit union idea caught on like a C-major chord. The credit union was chartered in 1960, although rumor says there was a slight delay while incredulous authorities investigated further. Tiny Treasurer Ruth Reid, who turns back the sleeves of her singing robes and conducts credit union business across a basement table after rehearsals, reports that the Musichorale Credit Union passed $5,000 in assets after a little more than a year of operation. At present, loans are below average, and the members as a group are saving their money with exceptional zeal. There's a good reason. The big plan, Ruth Reid confides, is for the entire Musichorale to fly to Europe. The credit union hopes to lend each member enough so that they can charter their own plane out of Chicago. Everybody around Chicago hopes they make it. And of those who know the story of Musichorale, Inc., and its credit union, few doubt that they will.

But if you believe that this must be the most "different" credit union in all Chicago, you are in error. You still haven't heard about the credit union in the cemetery.

Actually, this credit union serves a community of 15 Catholic cemeteries in Greater Chicago. The St. Anthony Guild Credit Union of Hillside, Illinois, has been called the White-Collar Grave Diggers Annual Picnic Society. The latter try at facetiousness has a tinge of the factual. Somewhere near one-third of the Guild's 250 regular employees and most of its 50 seasonal employees take pride in their necessary and deftly updated vocation. For the most part they operate tractor-mounted mechanical diggers which open a grave in one hour or less. Thus, by definition, St. Anthony's is an industrial credit union.

Functionally, it is a most unusual one. Since the member cemeteries are scattered over an area some 75 miles in diameter, the key man or sexton of each cemetery is an ex-officio director representing his own employees as well as the credit union as a whole. The Association has a remarkably liberal array of employee benefits, including holidays and insurance. But the Association regards the credit union, with about 70 per cent of all employees active members, as the ultimate in employee benefits. Most of them attend the credit union's annual picnic and outing for members. The president describes it as a family style gathering—"little but in big ways."

St. Anthony's Guild Credit Union made loans totaling nearly half a million dollars during the first seven years; losses were barely $500. The loan average rose from $366 in 1953 to about $1,515 in 1960. A painstaking and continuing record has been kept of the use of these loans. During 1960, a reasonably typical year, the tally stood as follows:

| | |
|---|---|
| 1. Automobile purchase and repair | 37 per cent |
| 2. Home improvement | 33 per cent |
| 3. Home furnishing and appliances | 7 per cent |
| 4. Insurance and gifts | 6 per cent |
| 5. Vacations | 6 per cent |
| 6. Consolidated bills | 3 per cent |
| 7. Medical expenses | 3 per cent |
| 8. Tuition | 3 per cent |
| 9. Taxes | 1 per cent |
| 10. Clothing | 1 per cent |

How continuous this listing may be is conjectural. But the unpaid directors of St. Anthony's Guild feel that some changes are due in terms of use of loans. They feel for example that 37 per cent for buying and maintaining autos is excessive. While recognizing that car ownership is essential to most of their members, they agree that shifting some part of the "auto bulge" to other uses is desirable and they believe attainable. They hope by techniques of counsel and discussion to bring about a gradual reduction of auto loans and a comparable increase of loans for tuition and school expenses, consolidated bills, and home improvements.

The leadership, which takes pride in its amateur status,

agrees that the member borrowers have a complete right to decide how they will use their loans. It also believes that counseling betters the use and ultimate values of the loans, and the service and the worthwhileness of the credit union.

This belief is expressed in simpler and more graphic terms by Jack Cotlow, a fireman in the Chicago "South Works" of U.S. Steel. Jack has played the hard steel game since 1938. Since 1945 he has been an active member, both in saving and borrowing, of the South Works U.S. Steel Credit Union.

This is one of the big industrial credit unions of our times. Like the big kangaroo it began small. In 1936 South Works closed its second year with assets of $28,000. In 1939, when Jack Cotlow paid his two-bit membership, and invested a first $5 in shares, credit union assets were up to $173,000. Steel was booming as 1939 ended. Steel was limping at half-capacity through most of the late '50's and beginning '60's. Yet during ailing 1960 the U.S. Steel Credit Union (South Works) edged past $5,000,000 in shareholdings.

Steel is a hard game and running a big steel credit union is no push-over either. Old-time Paymaster Harry C. Cramer, who carries on a second career as salaried treasurer of "Big Steel," is qualified to confirm the foregoing. He plays it safe, keeping $2,000,000 or more in ready cashable U.S. bonds against the ups and down he has learned to expect.

Jack Cotlow is no statistician. But he is not surprised to learn that nowadays his credit union makes about 6,800 loans yearly for a recent average of about $262.50

each. His own borrowings have averaged approximately that, with three notable exceptions.

The exceptions were "Harry Cramer handouts", specifically emergency loans designed to tide over between paydays or to meet calamitous needs; this with interest costs of approximately one thin dime. Routine loans were cleared punctually via the credit committee with loans delivered the following day, or at latest the following Monday. But Harry Cramer, as treasurer, holds and uses authority to grant emergency items. Accordingly, when Jack Cotlow's wife phoned that their then young son had fallen out of a tree and broken an arm, Jack had the doctors' and hospital fees in hand in two minutes flat. Another time Jack requested and received a quick-time loan after a losing encounter with a South Chicago pickpocket. And there was that time his wife won a TV prize contest and had to have instant cash to hire a trucker to bring home the spoils.

It is said that the Big Steel credit committee has never yet refused a properly entered loan application from an employee member with five years or more of seniority. Jack wouldn't swear to this. But he does vow that his credit union in general and Harry Cramer in particular bend over backwards for a member who needs help. Back in 1940, when Jack got quicksanded into a $600 hospital bill incident to the birth of Jack Jr., the proud father received a loan ten times the size of his shareholding. Having repaid the loan, Jack methodically built up his shareholding to $500 and presently more. Since then his successive loans have shaped a sort of personalized saga of financial progress: down payment on a building lot, birth of his daughter and his second son, his wife's operation, his own operation, his daughter's high school graduation, his daughter's wedding, successive years in college for both his sons, successive deaths of his wife's and his own parents, and a dozen other urgent and in great part noble obligations. In 21 years Jack Cotlow has never borrowed a dollar from a bank, a loan company, a relative or friend. He claims no medal for never having flunked a loan or bypassed an interest payment. Should medals be struck off for these honest deeds, Jack would pass them right along to the credit union and particularly to Harry Cramer.

By his own description, Harry Cramer is like any other industrial credit union treasurer. He grew up in steel, retired in 1957 after 24 years with U.S. Steel alone, and changed over from supervisor of the payroll department to full-time treasurer of the U.S. Steel South Works Credit Union.

The changeover wasn't too hard. Harry had been no-pay treasurer of the credit union since 1946, served eight years on its credit committee and two years as president. Earlier he had helped start two other successful steel workers' credit unions.

Harry Cramer hasn't entirely lost his Danish accent. He hasn't begun to lose his enthusiasm and his unbreakable affection for people. He has bailed his members out of jail, helped carry them to their graves, attended christenings of future members. He takes much advice, gives little, nags none. He rarely shows elation, never evidences despair. When strikes or shutdowns occur, "Old South Works" tranquilly notes, "We expect no payments until you are back at work."

"Steel is a hard business," Harry Cramer reiterates. "Hard but good . . . Things like strikes and layoffs it has to live with. Things like credit unions, it can't hardly live *without*. . . ."

Harry remains one of the everlasting amateurs.

# *Credit Unions and the Democratic Duty*

In terms of numbers the credit union is the fastest growing financial institution in the Western Hemisphere and much of the Eastern. In range of citizen participation and variety of uses it is the most versatile institution of our times. Accordingly there is no wholly typical credit union. But there are exemplary credit unions, and exemplary members who own them.

The following chronicle is a true story about one of them.

Jacques Chambrun has spent 40 years "lobsterin'" the aft coasts of Nova Scotia. Jacques' father, grandfather and great-grandfather before him also fished lobsters. In Nova Scotia this is an historic vocation which dates back to the early seventeenth century. Many of the first white settlers of the Maritime Provinces, in extensive "cold coast" areas an actual majority, had fished lobsters along various Old World seafronts even before migrating to the New. Most of the *Mayflower* passengers and for many years a majority of the Pilgrim Fathers were British Isles lobster fishermen.

Thus lobstering supersedes even fur trading as the most historic of North American enterprises. The trade started hard and stays hard. At least two previous generations of the Chambruns followed lobstering. Great-grandfather Henri lost his life while running a trapline in defiance of a hard-whipping October easter; Nova Scotia weather comes in many colors and sizes. But from season to season a good lobsterman scouts, sets and pulls his traps with reasonable regularity whether the sea chops foul or ponds fair. All too frequently in the old days of oar-propelled dories a man's feet or hands would freeze even before he could ably "fathom the chill." The sail dory proved a godsend in its time; nowadays the outboard motor is an even more effective expediter and lifesaver along the lobstering fronts.

Lobstering is still a trade for the independent. Working hard, silently and often dangerously, Jacques has remained with the trade and lived by it. He has lived better since 1938 when he joined the then infant St. Andrew Credit Union. The latter began in 1937 as a parish credit union with blessings and able help from the young vicar. But when the Protestant membership began outnumbering the Catholics, and when Scottish-descended fishermen and farmers from sparsely peopled upcoast settlements began clamoring for admission, the padre and his parishioners opened the door of welcome. At the second meeting the membership voted unanimously to replace the parish charter with that of a community credit union.

During his first lean year, Jacques invested every spare nickel and penny in shares and brought his passbook to a showing of $11.50. Lobstering went better the next year. Member Chambrun borrowed and promptly repaid a $40 loan, invested in laths, rope, buoys and the makings of 50 additional lobster traps. The following year he borrowed again to buy a new dory or open boat and a used outboard motor for it. Increased catch and improving prices justified the investment and within a few months he repaid the loan.

But the trade has other perils, financial and physical. In Nova Scotia, indeed all along the cold rocky shores and reef waters, down through the best proved offshore lobstering islands from New Brunswick's Deer Island far south, the lobsterman's earnings are traditionally scant. Skill, luck and good equipment are naturally important. But even with a good complement of all three, few working lobstermen net more than $2,000 a year; $800 to $1,200 is closer to average for the front as a whole.

Gross incomes are severely limited, too. The proprietor even of a good line of say 150 to 170 traps buoyed in first-rate locations does well to gross 75 cents per hour for his work. Though his working hours may shape a year-round average of close to twelve a day, a lobsterman who can turn in $4,000 in catch in any year is a superior brine farmer. For such an intake requires at least 20,000 pounds of catch; a fourth for discard as undersized; a tenth as "softers"; the rest for sea-front dealers offering prices which tend to range from 20 to 35 cents a pound at the pier. When local dealers or proprietors of lobster pounds are receiving 60 cents or more for quality product, the independent lobsterman does well to get 30 cents for his "legal prime" catch.

The disparity between the lobsterman's price and consumer's price (normally three times higher) is typical of ocean-front enterprises. Lobster is an exceptionally perishable quarry. Even in the best trapping locations discard ratios are high; at shedding times (the lobster sheds its shell each time it outgrows the crustaceous armor) wastes are excessive. And the prime catch involves very high handler's overhead which nowadays includes icing, crating, and air-expressing the live crustaceans. Most of the commercial catch is "pounded" or held in salt water tanks or sea edge ponds pending favorable markets which do not always materialize. In any case, feeding costs and confinement losses are substantial. Pre-cooked lobster meat is frequently a loss factor—all along the line.

Furthermore, the actual operation of lobster fishing is almost fabulously extravagant. Good locations are increasingly remote. The buyer and supplier or water front storekeeper is frequently the same person. He buys and sells rope, crating or ready-made traps, floats, bait, seins, boat fuel, repairs and supplies and the many other requirements in small quantities and at high overhead.

J. Chambrun's father "got through" and raised his family, as he noted, with the help of God and a "flight of angels hovering in me bowsprit." Also with the help of a self-operated garden farm which he sometimes fertilized with prime lobsters when nobody would buy them.

God was kind and angels continued to hover in the Chambrun bowsprit when Jacques Chambrun came home from the war, determined to get on with lobstering. He borrowed again, this time $300, as of that date, 1946, the biggest loan in the credit union's history.

Again the loan was good and the lobster catches and prices were above average. For a dozen more years Chambrun lobstered along, making the best of a hard and intermittently exciting trade. During those years he received and repaid fourteen loans from his credit union. They averaged around $80 each and in greatest part Jacques and his wife Kate used the money to furnish and improve their home, buy school supplies and pay parish school and college tuition for their four children. Their eldest daughter is now a registered nurse. Their first son is a railroad accountant with a college degree. Their younger son and daughter are away in schools.

About three years ago Chambrun faced up to a discrepancy which is basic not only to the industry of lobstering but, as the governors of the Bank of Canada note with eloquence and pertinence, to Canadian and Free World economy in general. This is the entrepreneur's nightmare of indirectness. Through a laborious four decades of lobstering Jacques had kept to pattern by spending approximately half of his gross take for necessary supplies, principally rope and trap lumber (both formidable expenses), boats, including repairs, motors and fuel, buoys, locker floats and so on. By year round averages the first two are the most debilitating. In the course of any year a lobsterman uses hundreds of pounds of rope—which must be brine-resistant, pull-resilient abacá, or Manila fiber.

As a beneficial alternative to piecemeal buying, Jacques organized a rope pool which enabled him and seven neighbors to purchase their rope needs at wholesale. Jacques financed the first nonprofit pool purchase with a credit union loan; after that the enterprise became self-sufficient.

When an exceptionally long and rugged winter provided an unsolicited abundance of leisure time, Jacques began home manufacture of lobster traps. These are five or six-sided slatted cages about four feet long and fifteen inches in diameter with a sealed end and a trap or funnel end. The latter features an aperture through which the lobster enters in quest of bait. In the old days most lobstermen built their own traps, felling the hardwood, splitting the laths and sawing the cooperage pieces. If it took a week to so fashion a dozen traps, that was all right; a lobsterman's shore time isn't worth much anyhow.

Jacques had built his share of traps, the hard, slow way. More recently he had bought the "mill mades" which never entirely satisfied his own exacting standards. So he rigged his otherwise unused barn as a workshop. That done, he turned again to his credit union for money to equip the shop. He invested $425 in a power adz and stationary ripsaw. A planer, bandsaw and rail-mounted push car completed the rudimentary equipment and brought the investment to about $1,600. Jacques was able to take about a fourth of the total from savings. He borrowed the rest from the credit union. This came easily because his share account covered the entire loan with a good $100 to spare.

For the first year Jacques contented himself with replacing about 75 of his old traps and adding 50 new ones to his line. Then he hired two helpers, one an experienced lumber-mill operator who works full time, the other a cooper who works half time. After the trio had produced and sold a first thousand traps in the course of four winter months, Jacques Chambrun devoted half the gross profit to improving the machinery and laying in a stock of rope, netting, nails and other accessory goods and used the rest of the profits for paying interest and melting down the loan balance.

In 1961, without extending sales efforts farther than ten miles along his home coast, Jacques settled his credit union loan in full, added another man to his factory force, pegged wages several dollars a week above the going average of the area and acquired a partner for his own lobstering operations.

At a young 56, Jacques confided that he felt he was coming of age both as a lobsterman and a backyard manufacturer. Recently when he attended his credit union's annual meeting to take over his new post as director, the farm-wife treasurer handed him a letter from a director of a pioneer Newfoundland credit union and co-operative. The letter contained an order for five cords of lathing and 500 assembled traps, all for sea shipment prepaid by buyer. After the business meeting and a pleasantry of cake and tea, the new director was called on to speak a few words regarding his personal views of credit unions.

Jacques rarely speaks more than a few words on any occasion, but this was a special occasion. The old-timer began by noting that St. Andrew's is still a little credit union. Its present assets are about $18,000. But no worthy loan applications are being refused and few are reduced in amount. "It's not the bigness that counts. It's the helpfulness."

Jacques also notes that credit unions have come up rapidly in the Maritimes. It takes eight to ten years for a lobster to reach market size. Plenty of credit unions, including his own, have fallen into working stride in less than a fourth that time. In 1931 when Roy Bergengren, the great evangelist for North American credit unions, first came to Nova Scotia to tell about credit unions, on invitation of St. Francis Xavier University, Jacques Chambrun was already 27 and had been lobstering his way for 13 years. There are now well over 450 credit unions in the Maritime Provinces. The innovation has long since spread from Nova Scotia to Newfoundland, Prince Edward Island and New Brunswick, thence to every province of Canada.

Thirty years earlier, credit unions had already come to the Acadian lands of Quebec in another form. There these earlier institutions were developing under the name of *Caisses Populaires,* or people's banks. This name is misleading. In no form are credit unions banks, as we understand the term today. Nor are they unions in the sense of being labor unions. Credit unions are co-operative saving and lending societies.

Credit unions had still earlier forebears, which date back more than a century to the first community-wide defense against economic evils, born when hard times were tormenting, even destroying tenant farmers and other peasants in South Germany. The name then was Raiffeisen Societies. Their founder, Friedrich Wilhelm Raiffeisen, was a minister and long time mayor of Flammersfeld. As mayor, lay pastor and a self-designated keeper of his brethren, Friedrich Raiffeisen sought to establish an effective defense against a cruel and useless usury which was destroying the solvency of his people. The persisting scarcity of credit was keeping his parishioners at the status of starvelings.

The Raiffeisen philosophy of creating credit was linked with the founder's concept of "practical Christianity" . . . "The Christian loves his fellow man," Raiffeisen reasoned. "He does not wish him harm, and he helps the poor and the needy. And the Christian helps with self help." The Raiffeisen Society of and for oppressed tenant farmers and other countryside laborers, was a community venture in the co-operative establishment and use of self-made credit facilities.

The founder noted: "We have been able to obtain the necessary money everywhere, even if only very gradually . . . as long as dependable, competent and inspiring people have headed a credit union . . . *The good Lord does not allow that Christian duty be bought off by financial contributions, no matter how large.* We must be effective by setting a living example. The Christian faith must regain its influence, and Christianity must regain its respect. There is only one way to do this—to demonstrate sincere Christian faith through charity. Credit unions are an excellent means to this end. . ."

The founder's concept of the credit union as a living and working instrument of practical Christianity has endured throughout most of the Christian world and beyond. So has the founder's insistence that the credit union must stand against economic trends which would separate people into but two groups, millionaires and beggars, and that it must therefore increase and strengthen the middle classes by "raising members of the impoverished class." In this and other of its definitive philosophies the credit union has been able to serve and correlate and justify its being among members or devotees of every principal religion of mankind, including Christian, Jewish, Buddhist, Mohammedan and other great faiths of West and East.

Thousands of credit unions are now directly associated with specific churches. Still more thousands are vitally related with specific governments and existing banking structures. Yet in all instances the credit union has been able to endure as a separate and distinctive entity: a lawfully authorized, duly chartered, non-subsidized citizens' association for saving, borrowing, lending, insuring, and earning. In all instances its members are its only owners. Its capital is of the true savings and earnings of the owner-members, not of synthetic papers or nominal stocks. Unlike banks, its net earnings go directly to its customers who are also participating members and owners.

The credit union's rate of dividend payment is democratically determined. As a rule these dividends range from two to five per cent, with three to four per cent near average, but by total, range from less than one per cent to six. By similarly democratic process and in keeping with sovereign law a credit union also establishes its own interest rates, almost universally limited, however, to a maximum of one per cent per month on the actual unpaid balance of loan. Another steadfast principle is that credit union loans are made without penalty of fee or any extra charges. Membership fees are nominal; in the United States they are usually 25 cents per member, though they may be even less. If and as they see fit, members may establish a maximum on shareholdings, but the general and prevalent trend is away from fixed or absolute limits.

Contemporary credit unions adapt readily to all types

of associated member groups, such as residents of a given community, members of a given congregation, or club, or fraternal order, employees of the same company or corporation or shop, factory, store, or government service, or fellow members of a given profession, such as teachers, physicians or dentists, farmers and so on. By basic philosophy as well as specific charter terms, racial or any other integration is far advanced in credit unions and clearly destined to be all-prevalent. In terms of credit responsibility as well as professional, business, and social relationships of members, discrimination on a basis of race or color, or ancestry or religion is contradictory to fundamental principles and economics, as well as social justice. The credit union can be valid only as living and working democracy.

Each credit union must hold an annual meeting open to all members. In practice and by charter agreement all members may, indeed are, duty bound to participate in the regular and democratic election of officers, including directors and key committee men or committee women, who in those capacities serve without pay. By process of membership vote, a credit union may employ for pay either part time or full time workers or both, to conduct its business. But most credit union work is still done gratis by members and/or their duly elected officers.

By implicit obligation each credit union must operate independently, serving its members above all other interests and serving all impartially. The credit committee is duty bound to weigh the credit status and expressed needs of each borrower individually. The borrower's character remains the basic consideration for any loan application; his signature is the basic security. All credit union officers and committeemen are foresworn to hold members' affairs in strictest confidence and to refrain from using elective authority for personal gain or advantage.

A majority of credit unions are officially chartered by the state or province in which they operate. In the United States almost half of all credit unions are currently chartered under state law, slightly more than half under federal law. All Canadian credit unions are chartered under laws of their respective provinces. In other nations, most operate by authority and under supervision of a specific statute or succession of statutes pertaining to credit unions, or similar financial co-operatives, though a few remain under general laws governing co-operatives.

Like banks, credit unions must submit to periodic examination of books and records by duly prescribed government authorities. In the case of the United States, credit unions like banks are subject to laws and regulations enacted by Congress as well as the respective state legislatures and to executive orders of the President. Unlike banks, credit unions are obliged to be self-provident in terms of various routine services which federal or state governments, or both, provide for banks. At their own expense and choice most credit unions belong to credit union leagues which are supported wholly by voluntary payment of dues. Credit union leagues operate on a state basis in the United States; in other countries by provinces or similar divisions.

The function of the credit union league includes helping organize new credit unions; providing management assistance to credit union officers and employees; sponsoring schools and conferences concerned with credit union work and problems; providing forms and supplies; and in some instances operating central credit unions for augmenting credit resources of individual member groups and providing services to credit union officers ineligible for full loan service in their own credit union. The Credit Union National Association at Madison, Wisconsin, is also the international association for credit unions throughout the world.

The credit union movement is becoming increasingly global. It gains impressively in Australia, reaches boldly into liberated Africa and into practically all of Latin America where the credit union gains luster as one of the brighter hopes for the survival of free enterprise, defense against Communism and blighting dictatorships, and the upbuilding of middle and lower classes. In Mexico and most of the Caribbean countries credit union gains are impressive, and as elsewhere, intimately tailored to citizen needs.

The credit union movement also gains steadily in Japan, Pakistan and India, also in Thailand, Malaya and the Philippines Republic, and by way of the Fiji Islands and American Samoa in other areas of the South Pacific. Gains in Western Europe, the British Isles and Scandinavia also press ahead. In terms of percentage of total census now holding active membership in credit unions, Canada remains a world leader.

The United States leads in total membership and resources. A century plus after the founding of the first Raiffeisen Society near Flammersfeld, Germany, late in

1849, the United States had more than 21,000 duly chartered credit unions with more than 13,000,000 members representing all 50 states, the District of Columbia and Puerto Rico.

In New York State, for instance, credit unions in the summer of 1962 were reported more numerous and more affluent than ever, with a record of $229.9 million of loans outstanding on their books at the midyear. Assets of these institutions, now numbering 1,072, reached an all-time high of $311 million as the share investment of 722,325 members climbed to $270 million.

The credit union tides are steadily, at times rapidly, even tumultuously rising. The patterns of group associations are also changing. In the United States industrial credit unions are the most numerous. Percentage-wise, the other principal categories include credit unions serving government employees, transportation and utility workers, professional people, school teachers and school employees, church congregations and parish residents, food processors, wholesale and retail business employees, and members of labor unions.

In Canada, by neighborly contrast, the highest percentage of credit unions are residential or community; the next highest have memberships based on church or parish associations. Communism bars credit unions. In the free world as a whole, as in Canada, community credit unions and those related to church endeavors and services are fastest gaining.

The expanding story of credit unions in the United States dates back to 1909. But it remains a story of pioneering, including all of the trials and toils of pioneering. Among these are growing pains—related to the feat of reaching living and self-propelling size. Yet any credit union which capably fulfills bona fide needs for any bona fide group, even of limited potential, is almost never doomed to excessive or continuous littleness.

In numbers and "per cents," credit unions are the fastest growing of all U.S. financial institutions, although banks and others continue to push far ahead in dollar amounts, and to widen the gap each year. A similar pattern prevails for credit unions in other nations. But as Jacques Chambrun states it, "It's not the bigness that counts."

The most challenging need, both within home boundaries and beyond, is not for bigger credit unions but for many more of them—new credit unions in which every member knows every elected officer not only by surname but by nickname, and more importantly by handclasp.

# *Credit Unions and the Yankee Crusade*

The frontiers of credit unions have now spread about as far north and south as people live. This has resulted only because the individuals who conceive, establish, and directly serve credit unions are dedicated believers in them as instruments of public good. Explain it how you will, credit unions make their appeal to emotions and convictions which are deeply rooted in human experience. The compelling response they have evoked in so many thousands of people is among the most striking chapters in the credit union story.

This was true of Roy Bergengren, the plump, kindly-faced man who became the tireless apostle, evangelist and cross-country legalizer of credit unions in the United States.

Roy's father was the runaway son of a titled Swedish family. He fled to Massachusetts to escape reprisals for his outspoken criticism of vested privilege at home. After working two years as a common crewman on a fishing schooner shipping out of Gloucester, Charles Bergengren came ashore and applied for admission to Harvard Medical School. To his grateful astonishment he was accepted as a student, given shelter, diligent instruction and presently a succession of scholarships which enabled him to complete the hard driving four-year study course.

With his M.D. in hand, the refugee Swedish nobleman returned to Gloucester, set up practice as the "Fisherman's Doctor" and became a citizen of the United States. His office just back of the Gloucester piers became a haven for schooner men, slooper, trawler and lobstermen with desperate needs and little or no money. Doctor Charlie attended sick men in their fish-smelling schooner bunks, treated the wounded in open dories, visited offshore islands to attend wives and children of the fishermen. Without benefit of hospital facilities he became an able obstetrician and his successes as a ship-deck surgeon are still legend along the Gloucester fishing front.

Later Doctor Charlie married and moved his family to Lynn, Massachusetts, where youngest son Roy was to graduate with honors from the Lynn Public High School. Roy left from Old North Station, aboard a lamplighted day coach, heated by a monkey-stove for the ten-hour trip to White River Junction, Vermont; thence, via river ferry and horse-coach he traveled to Dartmouth College.

After four years at Dartmouth, Roy in 1903 won his Bachelor's Degree plus a notation in the college yearbook as the "Class Member Most Likely to Succeed–in an Argument." Finally, with his father's approval, Roy applied for and won admission to Harvard Law School.

After graduation in 1906, the young man passed the bar in Massachusetts, returned across the Charles and set up a modest law office in his home town, Lynn. Young Roy's entry into law showed marked similarities to his father's entry into medicine. On all sides he found the poor and the aggrieved with many troubles and little money. Like his father, Roy Bergengren promptly established a professional name as a champion of the down-and-outers and an exceptionally ineffectual fee collector.

But the shoe workers and other sweatshop victims needed help, and Roy Bergengren, Attorney-at-Law, gave them help. Unemployment was chronic. Tenements were deplorable. Bars were flourishing, as were the local loan sharks. Young Roy saw tenement homes raided bare by chattel mortgage foreclosures, and served clients who, since they were already paying interest at the rate of 25 per cent per month on loan obligations, naturally couldn't pay lawyer fees. He saw and smelled other developments which cried out for corrective efforts. For instance, most of the saloons were owned either by the shoe-making companies or the tenement owners, which in several instances were one and the same.

Roy worked hard for the good of the needy, and as with his father, Cupid presently invaded the tangled skeins of his works. It happened that a young and pretty Yankee girl, Gladys Louise Burroughs, was rooming with Roy's younger sister at the Wheelock Normal School in New Jersey. It happened, too, that Roy met his sister's pretty roommate and liked her. On second meeting he liked her even more, and in 1910 after Gladys began teaching in the East Orange Public School system, Roy found need for extending a New York business trip to include East Orange. Rather breathlessly he called at her boarding house and asked for a word with her. The word was that Gladys Burroughs had been made for Roy Bergengren.

Counsel did not wait cross questioning since he was

obliged to make a train. He made the train and continued the courtship by mail. The couple met in person a total of three times during Gladys' two years of teaching. They were married in 1911 and returned to Lynn where both were aware that if they were to eat regularly certain professional changes were in order. After a brief but unsuccessful entry into the coal business, Roy moved into municipal politics.

Lynn, Massachusetts, was one of the first American cities to adopt the commission form of municipal government. Roy Bergengren chose, and after a valiant campaign won, the crucial office of Commissioner of Finance. The "Shoe Making Capital of America" was in need of some enlightened finance. The reasons included bad police work. Much of the prevailing crime was being incubated in the gin mills. Roy Bergengren opposed liquor. Though he came of a family of moderate imbibers, the new Finance Commissioner saw nothing good coming from saloons which were being used to steal back employees' pay. He said so openly.

The crusading commissioner kept on fighting to clean up his home town. He did not win all his battles. But he did not lose easily nor uniformly, and the opposition remembered the frays a long time. However, four years of the rough-and-tumble left him with scars and bruises. Late in 1916 Roy Bergengren suffered what his doctors termed a complete physical breakdown. This led to major surgery, removal of appendix, gallstones and a bladder section. But the stubborn cross between Yankee and Swede survived. The survival led Roy to two formative experiences, both in 1917.

He met and formed a warm friendship with Boston's remarkable merchant prince and civic advancer, Edward Filene, whom Bergengren privately described as a "most exciting cross between God and Satan." In his own way Filene was inclined to return the title, even while hiring, discharging and invariably re-employing Bergengren as his "special attorney." Filene had followed the stormy career of Lynn's Commissioner of Finance and sensed that Bergengren was headed on a "pathway of destiny."

When the First World War came, Bergengren volunteered for service in the U.S. Army, although crowding 38. After a mail-watching month Bergengren was commissioned a Captain of Ordnance and assigned to the First Army Base in Boston. As a recalcitrant assignee to the desk-and-wastebasket brigade, Captain Bergengren applied diligently and eloquently for combat duty overseas. The Army responded by issuing him an extra telephone and two additional wastebaskets. The Captain continued to apply for transfer to the Western Front, but Armistice Day found him still fighting the battle of the mimeographs. At least he had learned a great deal about paper work.

Back in Lynn, Massachusetts, where the shoe industry was backsliding dangerously as military purchases diminished, he joined the throngs of service men seeking to readapt themselves to civilian lives and earnings. While reviving remnants of law practice, Roy Bergengren stumbled upon what looked like a valid business opening, the contract manufacture of fine candy kisses for an old Boston confectionery firm. The intentions were good and so were the candy kisses, thanks in part to the professional skill of H. Higgins, British candymaker. The war had boomed the candy trade, but it had also boomed the price of sugar, principal ingredient of quality kisses. Candy prices fell, but sugar stayed aloft.

The enterprise didn't exactly fail; it slurped away sweetly. And Roy Bergengren had learned that "enterprise capitalism" cannot live without credit. Having written off his losses, he shouldered his debts and journeyed to Boston to make a call on Edward Filene. The merchant prince mentioned a vacancy in the management of the Massachusetts Credit Union Association. "I accepted with alacrity," Bergengren recalled, "and went home to my wife and children wondering what a credit union was."

Next day on reporting for work at Room 23, 5 Park Square, Boston, he began to find and build his own answer. The year was 1920. Room 23 was the incubator of the credit union national movement in the United States. The man who was to be the most formative of American credit union personalities had found at last the right place to hang his hat. The Massachusetts Credit Union Association grew into the Credit Union National Extension Bureau, and the now international Credit Union National Association in Madison, Wisconsin.

Bergengren's first venture in organizing a specific credit union took place in Gloucester. His first venture in organizing what became the nation's first credit union "chapter" was also in Massachusetts—at Springfield. Of perhaps comparable significance, the first acquisition of credit union office equipment occurred in 1920 when Bergengren tripped over an abandoned typewriter which a secretary had left on the floor of Filene's Washington

Street office. Bergengren subsequently used this machine to draft some 35 bills which became credit union laws in as many states.

The first Bergengren work goal for credit unions, which crowded sixteen astonishingly busy years was: "Get the Laws." During 1909 Massachusetts had acquired the nation's first statute authorizing credit unions. Five years later, in the second year of his Presidency, William Howard Taft had written to all governors urging their support of credit union laws similar to Massachusetts'. But after three years only three states, New York (via the then state senator, Franklin Delano Roosevelt), North Carolina and Rhode Island, had legislated usable acts to authorize the founding of credit unions.

Beginning in 1921, Bergengren launched works which contributed or led to credit union laws for Virginia, Kentucky, Indiana and Tennessee, and in time Nebraska, New Jersey, Mississippi and Louisiana. By 1925, thanks in great part to Bergengren's legal competence and inspired stubbornness, plus his exceptional talents for recruiting companions in the crusade, the credit union movement was flowering into interstate reality. The Boston Postal Employees Credit Union reported a then almost incredible total of 700 active members. The American credit union progress was being viewed around the world from Belgium to New South Wales. Also during 1925 Illinois, Iowa, Minnesota and Michigan joined the fold of legislative approvers, the monthly publication *Bridge* materialized, and Chicago's first credit union (Belden Manufacturing Company Employees) came into being.

Beginning in 1925 and continuing for a dozen years

thereafter the Bergengren work diary and letters comprised a revealing American saga of working hard and winning believers.

"I celebrated St. Patrick's Day (1927) with Father Roney at Dougherty, Iowa. After a preliminary meeting with him I went back taking a night train to Davenport at Marble Rock, where the train was flagged for me. I got to Davenport at 3 A.M. and put in a fruitful day. An interurban train got me from there to Clinton, Iowa, in time for a 1:40 A.M. connection back to Dougherty where I arrived at 7:20 A.M. . . . The wind was howling across the prairie . . . about noon it began to snow . . .

"In order not to waste the day I bummed a ride to Mason City about fifty miles all told. I organized the postal employees there and then the same obliging soul (Father Roney) took me back to Dougherty. This place has a population of about 200 and my next job was to visit the sixteen folks who had earlier promised to attend the second meeting (to discuss forming a credit union). Father Roney and I made the round of calls together, plowing through the rapidly increasing drifts. What we didn't know until later was that the local banker was shadowing us, visiting each place as we left and reminding the people that the bank held the papers of most of them and wouldn't like it if they went to Father Roney's meeting. When the hour of the meeting came Father Roney and I sat by a red-hot pot-bellied stove in his little study and waited. Nobody came. . . ."

But Bergengren proceeded to thousands of additional meetings where many did come to found and presently build credit unions, and to legislate acts which opened ways for tens of thousands more credit unions. On a wintry day in 1927 the unwavering crusader noted:

"Father Campbell arranged some parish meetings in Iowa. It was cold and rainy and we had tire trouble and got lost. However, we organized four new parish credit unions. . . . Another year (1927) had ticked away. We had been six years at it. We had twenty-three (state) laws which would work well, and two that wouldn't work at all. We had credit unions in twenty-six states and were in contact with interested people in all the others. There were credit unions, a thin line of them, to be sure, but they extended from Portland, Maine, to Los Angeles. Above all, we were finding men—Howell, Doig, O'Shaughnessy, Long, Rentfro and many others, the privates in the crusade who were earning their commissions. . . . In the credit union movement we do not expect the general to lead from a desk chair fifty miles behind the front lines. In February, for example, on one twenty-day trip I covered twenty cities and towns of seven states and with much local help everywhere, organized twenty-nine additional credit unions. . . ."

Bergengren also toured Europe and studied credit unions in Czechoslovakia, Switzerland and Sweden, homeland of the Bergengrens . . . "Everywhere I found people united in their determination to improve their economic lot through co-operative actions. . . . The Raiffeisen Societies were, I found, close to the people they serve. They reached down and lifted up . . . They humanized the control of money, a process greatly needed in our own American democracy. . . ."

Back in America where (as of 1929) the word "thrift"

was fast becoming obsolete, the crusader resumed and amplified his expanding labors to found credit union leagues and to "get the laws." Legislative and organizational work improved as the roaring '20's quieted down and the sober '30's took over. New workers and great companies joined the crusade which reached farther in all directions—north to Nova Scotia and south to Georgia.

It was 1931 when Roy Bergengren began his perceptive exploration of Canadian credit unions. He was in good hands and he kept to significant places. These included Antigonish, St. Francis Xavier College, and the fundamental Nova Scotian hinterlands and sea fronts which have incubated, raised up and exported so much of the credit union philosophy to many nations and races of man. Some called it the "Antigonish movement." It was and is non-denominational, moldable to specific human needs, ready to work for and with all people of good will.

What presently emerged as the Antigonish movement began with a pioneer meeting at Broad Cove Schoolhouse. Bergengren, A. B. MacDonald and Father Coady advanced to the place of meeting in a blinding snowstorm. One after another they saw other travelers emerging from the storm. "They seemed to be struggling through the drifts in the same general direction we were going," Bergengren recalled. "The schoolhouse was stone cold, but there was a big, pot-bellied stove and plenty of wood, and so we organized the first credit union in Nova Scotia and christened it the Filene Credit Union. . . ." Others were destined to follow.

Bergengren knew, of course, about the work in Canada

of Alphonse Desjardins, who brought the first credit unions to Levis, Quebec, in 1900. Desjardins had also helped to establish the first credit union in the United States in 1909 at Manchester, New Hampshire. At Filene's invitation, he had also come to Boston to testify at legislative hearings preliminary to passage of the Massachusetts law in 1909. The credit union structure prescribed by that law, and by virtually all subsequent laws governing credit unions, was based substantially on the credit society devised by Desjardins.

Alphonse Desjardins was a legislative reporter and self-educated economist. What he set up in his home village of Levis was based on his studious reading about credit clubs or "societies" which were flourishing not only in Germany, but in France, Holland, Belgium, and Scandinavia during the 1890's. Desjardins preferred the name *Caisse Populaire,* or People's Bank. His first practical venture began with an initial deposit of a dime, risked by a little girl of the neighborhood. Presently, the girl's parents, along with a carpenter, a pipefitter, and a joiner, saw fit to join the organization and raise its working capital to $28.31.

This initial experiment was carried forward at personal risk by Desjardins, who was held responsible for the entire assets under then existing law. It was followed in the course of years by notable successes.

*Caisses Populaires* in the St. Lawrence Valley today number more than 1,250. They remain distinctively French-Canadian, and are in the main, ably associated with the Catholic Church, its parishes and people. Though they have many points in common with other credit unions, the peoples' banks are more strongly traditional. As a rule they tend to restrict loans to staples and necessities, with strong emphasis on real estate loans.

Like other credit unions, the Caisses have flourished by meeting the workaday needs of members. Canada's commercial banks are severely limited in numbers and operate under Dominion charter. Sizable towns have branch banks, but villages and smaller towns are usually without national bank services. The gap has frequently been filled by a *Caisse Populaire* headquartered in the rectory, church basement, or an adjacent location, much as credit unions have met such needs elsewhere.

The desperate year of 1932 saw Edward Filene's entry into public arenas as a defender of credit unions. Perhaps slightly tongue-in-cheek Bergengren noted the tendency to lift, "for at least a little, the bushel off our credit union light . . . this by bringing Filene to the people. . . ."

As history was soon to prove, the Great Depression ushered in a magnificent era of credit union utility. The cause was augmented by the progressive failure or lawful suspension of 14,344 U.S. banks and presently by the Roosevelt bank moratorium of March, 1933 which included credit unions. "Now," Bergengren mused, "at the one time in all history when it was no compliment to be called a bank, our credit unions were banks by inference. We are having no runs and we did not want to be closed. . . ."

But throughout the United States credit unions were permitted to open the instant the holiday was legally endable. Thus they proved not only fundamental solvency but the already remarkable competence of their leagues and leaders. Meanwhile, the legislative gains, both on a state and national levels, continued to flower as the Roosevelt years followed.

In Madison, Wisconsin, during February, 1935, the newly formed Credit Union National Association held its first meeting in a typical February snowstorm. It replaced the Credit Union National Extension Bureau and moved the center of credit union activity from the Atlantic seaboard.

Meanwhile, the provincial legislature of Nova Scotia in 1932 enacted what is frequently referred to as the first of the "modern" credit union governing laws. This enactment was preceded by the Province of Quebec legislation of 1906. But Nova Scotia's enactment of 1932 is still regarded as especially cogent in terms of the basic principle of the credit union movement as it now lives and grows. Provincial enactments followed in New Brunswick and Prince Edward Island in 1936; Ontario, Saskatchewan and Manitoba in 1936; Alberta and British Columbia in 1938; Newfoundland in 1939; and during 1940 the British Columbia Credit Union League became the first provincial league to formally join the Credit Union National Association of Madison, Wisconsin. Credit union ties between Canada and the United States and the hemisphere at large continue to expand and strengthen.

By 1935 the formative years were ended. The promised land was arriving. On August 16, 1935, too, the CUNA Mutual Insurance Society formally began business as a cooperative rags-to-riches story with a $35,000 advance at four per cent from Edward Filene. Within a few years

CUNA Mutual had turned a minus $35,000 of assets into a plus of $1,000,000, with group coverage in force totaling billions, based on credit union shares and loans.

Beginning in 1941 all U.S. credit unions and most others "went to war," with Bergengren still heading the U.S. credit union forces. But the battle lines remained more human than military. By 1941 six states had more than 400 credit unions each. Credit unions were serving people in every corner of the continent. At Cross Lake, Manitoba, 49 Cree Indians who lived in a community reachable only by canoes had organized their own successful credit union with $600 in shares, all saved from trapping and fishing!

Summing up credit union accomplishments in Canada, original organizer A. B. MacDonald reported, "The story of water turned to wine is hardly less astounding than this modern miracle of beer become butter. In community after community the squandered cents are now savings; the bartender has been replaced with a treasurer. . . ."

Well after V-J Day and his spectacularly active "retirement" to a Green Mountain farm on the old Berlin Road out of Montpelier, Vermont, Roy Bergengren closed his book, *Crusade,* with "Whatever the problems of this troubled world, one thing is certain: With God's help—in the end man will be free."

To this remarkable man in blue serge, all his career work of founding credit unions has been a crusade. That is still his story. Roy Bergengren died on Veteran's Day, 1955. His crusade presses on throughout the Free World. His modestly marked grave in the little corner cemetery on the Berlin Road symbolizes the unselfish modesty of the cause. But there is no end of the spirit, the personality, or the art of leadership or the living cause of credit unions which Roy Frederick Bergengren espoused, symbolized and brought into being.

4

# *Credit Unions and the Need to Grow*

Credit unions are many things to many people. But to most members, the great majority of credit unions are living assemblies which depict and delineate American environments, geographic, economic and temperamental.

In the past, practically all American enterprises were marked and indeed permeated by regional characteristics; many still are. The village or general store of New England, for example, showed and still shows implicit contrasts to the village or general store in the Deep South, or the Pacific Northwest, or the Southwest Atlantic. Not even our expanding era of chain stores can erase the distinguishing regional qualities of the member stores.

Credit unions are particularly disposed toward regional distinctions, regardless of size or numbers. Through the years, definite characteristics of credit unions keep moving with, adjusting to, and taking form from definitive places, including certain profoundly revealing American heartlands. Consider, therefore, the story told by Henry Lindbergh Peterson. Henry would not call himself a celebrity and certainly not a hero to a cause. But he does happen to be the first citizen to win federal civil status as a credit union organizer, with the somewhat baffling but official title of Junior Credit Union Investigator.

Henry Peterson took up farming in drought-parched Western Kansas at the impressionable age of ten. In 1905, Henry's Danish farmer parents emigrated from the old country and homesteaded a "double quarter" (320 acres) out on the buffalo or short grass flats a half-day's wagon drive from Dodge City, one-time home of Marshal Dillon and rail terminal for the great cattle drives. There the Petersons broke sod, raised a cabin and pole barn and began growing wheat. Their son Henry, who presently became American-speaking, took to the plow and apron drill and worked hard to learn the great basic trade of Kansas, wheat.

Henry returned to his father's farm after service in World War I, just in time to see the Kansas-centered wheat boom trip and fall on its face. Henry's father died and the 320 acres would no longer yield a living, even for one man. Henry therefore set out to buy a bigger farm, 1,180 acres. He planted 200 acres to wheat and began raising beef cattle. The wheat grew tall and golden. Cattle thrived and fattened on buffalo grass. But markets continued to toboggan. U.S. farming in general, Kansas farming in particular, was in big trouble.

There had to be a way out. Partly from need, partly by ancestral tradition Henry Peterson began by turning to the old Scandinavian facility of the farmers' co-operative. Times were rough for organizing producers' co-operatives, but Henry and his neighbors organized wheat growers' co-ops, including a farm supply co-op and a co-operative grocery store. At the time Dodge City was an important railroad town and freight terminal, and its railroad workers quickly joined the move toward co-ops. Despite the waverings of international wheat markets, Dodge City began emerging as one of the eminent co-operative centers of the U.S. West.

Then the "all-benefiting circle of trade" began breaking apart. The first took the form of a prolonged railroad strike which the workers lost. That dealt jolting losses to the co-operative stores. Almost simultaneously came the great blowing plagues of wheat rust which obliterated hundreds of thousands of acres of prime flour wheat, and a succession of severe droughts which conspired to leave bins and elevators partly or completely empty. Then, along with worse droughts, came the Great Depression.

Like his country neighbors Henry Peterson kept on hoping for the best, raising wheat and co-operating. There was little else to do. But depression lingered, then got worse. After taking office on a calamitous fourth of March, 1933, Franklin Delano Roosevelt and his New Deal began launching a torrent of corrective legislation. The resulting grab-bag of economic laws and executive decrees included the nation's first barter sponsorship at federal levels, a liberalized farm credit act, and, in 1934, a law for federal sponsorship of credit unions.

Passage of the Shepard Bill assigned the administration of credit unions to the Farm Credit Administration. During the following May the U.S. Civil Service Commission announced and readied a first competitive examination for Junior Credit Union Organizer. News of the announcement reached Henry Peterson by way of

Henry Hargis, a Dodge City post office employee. Hargis urged his country neighbor to take the examination. So when the day came, Peterson went into the Dodge post office and took the examination along with 400 others. A few weeks later, he received a "score notice" from the Civil Service Commission. He put the paper on the mantlepiece and went back to harvesting wheat. When his post-office friend phoned to ask his score, Henry had forgotten it, but presently located the letter, which he read back. His friend whistled softly. "Sounds high to me, Henry."

It was. Henry Peterson had barely "elevated" the wheat when he received the news that he had been appointed the nation's first credit union organizer. Henry's first question was directed to himself. It was very simply, "Will democracy, which I believe in, work with and in credit unions?" After due thought he answered the question affirmatively. He has never changed his answer.

In a one-day stand in Washington, D.C., Peterson was assigned a territory which included Kansas, Colorado, Oklahoma, Arizona and New Mexico. His first six months was to be a probationary tryout. His working equipment included his own gently rusting auto with worn tires and a government-supplied brief case filled with mimeographed application forms.

During his day in Washington, Henry had been favored with a comprehensive two-hour lesson in keeping cash ledger sheets and making single-column entries in account books. Entrained home, he continued to fill out imaginary credit union ledgers for credit unions still unborn.

Brief case in hand and good intentions in mind, Henry set out on a new career. He headed first for what he knew most about, distressed farms and farmers. When he brought up his leading question, "How'd you like to have a credit union?" the almost invariable answer was, "What's a credit union?"

At Pueblo, Colorado, where Henry arrived as a result of misinterpreting a road sign, he succeeded in starting his first credit union—for a friendly but job-scared group of packing house workers. Encouraged, the junior investigator stopped at Santa Fe long enough to establish his second credit union and at Albuquerque, in a single day, he collected four applications for credit union charters, one for local school teachers, another for local newspaper employees, another for the local Veterans Hospital staff, the fourth for employees of the local power company.

After the big day at Albuquerque the Peterson progress reports grew fewer. During his entire year Henry succeeded in organizing or "seeding" only 37 credit unions; the chair warmers in Washington had set a minimum quota of organizing 100 credit unions in a year. But the following year, when the New Deal instated twelve more credit union organizers, Henry Peterson, quota flunker that he was, found himself designated as training officer for all the others. "Can't honestly say that I taught those men a dang thing," Henry reflects. "But I sure learned a lot myself while trying to teach 'em."

As he worked along, Henry Peterson became more and more convinced that the most needed credit unions are frequently hardest to "get off the ground." As he talked with farmers and weighed their credit problems, Henry kept reviving his earlier interests in farm co-operatives, also in town co-operatives with substantial rural memberships. One after another he restudied the shambles and survivals among co-operatives he had earlier known, including several he had personally helped organize or direct. For the most part they were just hanging on, like visiting relatives from Arkansas, yet even the feeblest had an enduring strength: they had won friends, earned followings, served communities, and converted people to the habit of working and serving together.

In a depression-ravaged farm scene, Henry Peterson therefore saw local co-ops as superior seedbeds for credit unions. One of his first successes materialized back home in Kansas at Hutchinson, then a farm center with about 30,000 people. Hutchinsonians and their country neighbors had already founded the storm-weathering Reno Co-op, which was ably serving both producers and consumers, on farms and in the town. The cluster of co-operative enterprises included purchase and resale of cattle feeds, also commercial fertilizers, petroleum products, staple farm supplies, and a co-operative dairy. On Groundhog Day, 1937, Henry Peterson called on the Reno directors and "sprung the idea" of organizing what promptly became the Reno Co-operative Federal Credit Union. The weather was not compatible for selling anything, not even an idea. The thermometer hovered at zero and a mixture of powder snow and sleet kept spitting against the frosted windows of the anteroom where the co-op board sat and shivered.

Even so, the directors voted yes and applied for a

charter which was promptly issued. With the credit union in work, the entire co-operative enterprise began taking a new lease on life. Directors and members alike began purchasing shares, in many instances changing nonproductive and emaciated bank accounts to small but productive credit union assets. One after another, good co-op customers who had been unable to pay their debts began borrowing from the credit union and paying them.

One after another, the Reno credit union succeeded in changing due accounts from mere merchandise receipts to orderly, dated, interest-yielding notes. Members began buying credit union shares, thereby reducing their interest costs. At present the Reno Co-op Credit Union is a model for Kansas or anywhere else, with more than 2,200 active members, well divided between town and country, and valid assets of around $1,500,000.

Word got around. So did Henry Peterson. Over in Garden City, about 54 miles west of Dodge City, another well organized co-operative was having severe depression pains. Garden City, Kansas, then with about 6,000 people, was a typical Great Plains wheat town. Its co-operative had begun well. Herb Clutter, its president, was an able businessman, a member of Federal Farm Credit boards who knew farm finance. He also knew the Garden City Co-op was holding about $85,000 in accounts receivable, but unreceived. Herb Clutter therefore saw a credit union as a green hope for the co-op's survival, as well as economic salvation for the members. He and his fellow board members voted unanimously to take the lead in organizing a farmers' and all-community credit union, promptly joined as first members and dug deep to buy the first $20,000 worth of shares. The resulting credit union took off well and never stopped. It is now one of the most progressive in Kansas, and a superb working model for any place.

Meanwhile Henry Peterson was perfecting an organizational technique which rarely fails. It is the neighborly get-together routine. Henry begins by sponsoring or causing others to sponsor a family dinner or supper meeting of apt-to-be interested farmers, townspeople, co-op workers, labor union heads and local employers at the home town hotel or a good restaurant. He makes a special point of asking in the county agricultural agent, the county home demonstration agent, the local bankers and all principal businessmen. After a good meal he presents his story simply and briefly, then invites questions and comments, being ready braced for hard questions, hard comments and highly localized considerations. Usually he hears the opposition dwindle as those assembled speak out.

At Colby, another of Kansas' wheat farming centers, the local farmers' co-op began to see merits in sponsoring a credit union for the use of its preponderantly rural clients. Lester Ludwill, the co-op president, volunteered to set up, and served as host for, the get-together dinner. Expecting bank opposition, Lester and Henry made a special point of personally inviting the president of the Thomas County National Bank. The bank president not only attended but spoke seven words by which he has meticulously abided, "My bank will work along with you." Within five years the Colby Credit Union was sound as a dollar and possessed of better than $150,000 in assets.

In wheat-rich, but then dollar-poor Johnson County, a group of about 150 wheat farmers was disposed to do some "chinning" about a community credit union to serve as a wheel horse for their producers' co-op, which had facilities for storing and selling several million bushels of wheat yearly, and a consumers' co-op which supplied groceries, gasoline, and other staples to the wheat-growing membership. At the first discussion session dinner, Henry Peterson was pleased to note that the local banker was not only present but was already on the board of directors of the co-operatives, and that most of the general membership was also on hand.

The members joined the directors in voting to apply for a credit union charter and to open a first account in the name of the combined co-operatives. Directors and employees together pledged a first purchase of credit union shares totaling about $7,000. On the day the charter was received, shareholdings were grown to well above $15,000. With the charter in hand the co-op's leadership urged the members to transfer their debts from the co-op to the credit union, and by doing so, to reduce the co-op's accounts receivable. As the co-op's credit union gained strength, it began standing and presently walking quite securely on its own feet.

Here as in several instances where rural credit unions which began quite literally as credit departments of local co-operatives, they shortly emerged durable and strong, with friendly associations with the original sponsor but a bona fide, self-sufficient credit union, each in its own right. As Henry Peterson worked along, the farmers' credit unions of Kansas and nearby heartlands began assuming similar statures and growth patterns. There is no preordained "right" size, though in general at least 200 members with assets of at least $75,000 fit the combination wheat-and-cattle farming best. Without exception the family touch of warm, personalized community interest so helpful to all credit unions is essential to the farmers'.

The Beloit (Kansas) credit union started with a community ice-cream "feed" to which everyone was invited. About 60 local children were among the early arrivers: more than half of them presently became members. Before all the ice cream was eaten the first, all-necessary $18,000 in shares had been bought. Other successful beginnings were associated with a fine old institution known as the Watermelon "feed". Box suppers proved another big help and still do, since they epitomize the tangible benefits of thrift and for good measure get the women into the act and interested. Organizer Peterson discreetly encouraged his own wife to make up box suppers.

He has also developed the strategy of spending suitable time and effort at preparing question boxes, directly concerned with credit unions. Any available box will do, such as shoe, dogwood or apple, with a slit in the top and a sign inviting everybody to write out their questions about credit unions and drop them in. Henry Peterson, whose blue Scandinavian eyes are frank and whose drawling words are unvaryingly forthright, has been known to fever the question boxes by dropping in a few key questions of his own. But after the socializing and refreshments are finished, Henry draws out all questions and does his best to answer them—briefly and candidly. For good measure he welcomes queries from the floor, or at outdoor meetings from the lawn, giving due heed to questions from children and women as well as the men.

Henry never favors relinquishing any crop once the seeds are sown. He grants that seeding, birth and youth are wonderful and necessary. But so, as any Kansas farmer will agree, are maturity and harvest.

Consider Grainfield, in western Kansas, which helps provide a still hungry world with millions of bushels of wheat every year. Grainfield, Kansas, has a farmers' and townspeoples' credit union which Henry Peterson helped get started. Not long ago Henry happened to drift by to attend its annual meeting. About 50 members were on hand with the makings of a promising box supper. Since there was urgent need for making more and larger loans available, a director recommended auctioning off the boxes for purchases of credit union shares; high bidder to share the box supper with the contributor and her next of kin. Henry Peterson "sort of expected" a favorably sized box supper might draw a bid of, say, five dollars' worth of shares. The first box supper on the auction table brought $350 in share purchases. Before the evening was finished the share balance was built up by about $7,000. The pie supper remains a classic Kansas institution which has responded ably to the cause of building credit unions for town as well as country use.

Henry Peterson quit his federal job back in the turning '40's to serve as managing director of the Kansas Credit Union League. More recently he has resigned from the post to return to his first calling of helping to found credit unions. In this endeavor he has worked with Mormons, Catholics, Baptists, Mennonites and other sectarian groups, with the Farmers' Union, Farm Bureau, all manner of professional and industrial groups.

For all groups the amount of credit needs continues to grow. For all groups, average loans have climbed steadily from less than $300 to more than $700, then to $900 and currently to about $1,500.

But loan averages for credit unions of grain and cattle farmers are soaring as operational costs reach and hold high plateaus. A modern tractor-powered wheat harvester costs around $8,000; a carload of feeder cattle between $10,000 and $12,000.

The farmer today is a business man who knows that having and using credit is essential. He must limit payment of interest to values producible from the loan. He strongly prefers to center all credit needs in a single loan and to amortize indebtedness following the sale of his principal crop or crops. It follows that the farmers' credit union must keep alertly in step with the changing tempos of farming needs. Kansas is a good place in which to pick up the pace.

Now and probably for many years to come, Kansas has the nation's highest ratio of farmers' credit unions. At the turn of the century a hard working farmer with sons or a hired man, and with plenty of plow horses, plows, harrows and seed drills could get along on a fair harvest of 200 acres of wheat with another 200 acres in "rest over" or reserve. But the coming of the mechanical harvester approximately doubled the average size of Kansas wheat farms. The great wheat boom set off by the First World War raised it another 25 to 50 per cent in acreage.

During the 1920's, hardening economics prodded a continued increase. By the dusty, stormy 1930's (in Kansas the phrase is "Dirty Thirties"), 640 acres or a square mile of wheat was the least from which any family could expect to eke a living. Nowadays two sections or 1,200 acres is the practical minimum.

But nobody could begin to "wheat farm" even one section without power equipment. A plowman afoot would do well to get around a mile-square field five times, or furrows, in a ten-hour day. With a standard type light tractor he can do better, but not nearly well enough. The need now is for heavy power rigs capable of drawing king-size equipment. A heavy tractor plus a suitably sized combine or harvesters and minimum equipment adds to about $13,000. Multiply by five or six and you arrive at the basic investment now centered in practically any workable wheat farm. Kansas lands are no longer cheap; taxes are no longer negligible; the tractor-power era is efficient and it is also expensive.

Farm credit unions must live with all these realities. They can no longer open shop with a few hundred dollars of paid-in shares, and thereafter grow like Topsy. It is proverbial, even in the smaller, most rural of farmers' credit unions, that an initial shareholding of $15,000 to $20,000 is minimum. As the local saying goes, the farmers' credit union must now be powered for "broad plowing with heavy pullers." It is a rugged condition, but like hundreds of rugged conditions which other kinds of credit unions are fulfilling, it is learnable and attainable. The farmers' co-operative has been the cradle and proving ground for the farmers' credit union. Time and time again the child has not only been the father of the man, but his lifesaver. This living, working pattern continues. The farmers' co-op, town and village members included, helps the credit union which helps, frequently saves, the co-op. Time and time again the co-operative's perennial debtors emerge as superb credit union members, borrowers, and owners. By the same processes of balance the co-operative's board of directors repeatedly emerges as the credit unions' best friends or most able leaders.

Here, obviously, is a mighty challenge for learning, teaching and doing—all important, many believe crucially important, because there is very good reason to believe that Kansas farming patterns as now centered on wheat and cattle, may be world patterns for good growing in years directly ahead. Henry Peterson, the first federal employee credit union organizer, is one of those still learning how the farmers' credit union can live with today's agriculture and build for tomorrow's.

It's a controversial subject. But as Henry says, any subject which cannot stand up to factual and honestly opinionated argument isn't much of a subject. Credit unions are.

# [ 5

# *Credit Unions and the Blue Collars*

About one-half the credit unions in the United States serve industrial employees. That means over 9,000 credit unions, including most of the larger ones. As any credit union field man can tell you, most of the obvious prospects among industrial plants already have credit unions in operation. CUNA estimates that the membership of these industrial credit unions adds up to something like 6,000,000 people, which is a pretty impressive slice of the wage-earning population, any way you choose to slice it.

In a typical manufacturing plant, the credit union gets started through the interest of company management, or the labor union, or both. Company management usually recognizes today that money worries are a prime cause of lost time, spoiled work, and even industrial accidents, an observation ordinarily supported by the pile of wage assignments and garnishments which harass the payroll office every month. In addition, there is the regular platoon of employees who come around for pay advances to head off similar troubles of their own. In most cases management, after any initial misgivings, is happy to see such annoyances passed along in large measure to an employee-owned organization ready to cope with them. In some plants, indeed, the credit union finds itself showered and embarrassed with well-meaning offers of help, out of pure gratitude. By contrast, the credit union is, at other plants, tolerated by the management only on condition that all its activities remain outside the gates. The typical situation falls somewhere between these two; a small space is cleared for the credit union in a corner of the plant, a space which it invariably outgrows. Thereafter, the credit union weighs the advantage of a convenient location in the plant against the advantage of finding its own quarters nearby. While in time many industrial credit unions ask for, and receive, payroll deduction privileges from the company, a few credit unions feel that they are actually "subsidized" by the fact that the company pays their electric light bill.

It is a fact of life for such credit unions that they are married to the fortunes of their company and their industry. They cannot take in members from outside, only those within the specific group named in the charter. The company's wage-earners are, in fact, the credit union. When times are bad for the company they are bad for the credit union. If the plant has 1,000 employees and sees fit to lay off 100 of them, it engineers a crisis affecting 10 per cent of the credit union's members. If the plant should fail or go out of business, the credit union has to liquidate, going into its reserves for the money to pay off the shareholders. Of all possible "subsidies" an industrial credit union might receive, the most necessary one is thus the continued success and prosperity of the company to which it is so inexorably tied. To separate the credit union from the industry, you first have to separate the members from their jobs.

Nowhere is this situation more strikingly revealed than

in the steel business, the greatest and most basic of all our industries. Above all else, the talent that made the United States a great industrial nation was its ability to extract metals from the earth; to mine, smelt, work, shape, and deliver the structural factors needed in the building of the economy. The ores were created by Providence in abundance throughout the land. The work force was recruited from a swelling population over a period of three centuries. Iron and steel have become so significant a factor in the nation that the fluctuating fortunes of the business are unquestioningly held to reflect the economic health of the country. Steel is repeatedly called the "barometer of industry."

It is easy to see why. Modern civilization, as the saying goes, is built on a base of steel. Name any item which satisfies your basic wants for food, clothing and shelter, and you will probably find it is made or transported with steel equipment. People? At least 700,000 people work in the processing plants of the iron and steel business, or in closely related trades. Furthermore, economists guess that no less than 200,000 different products are manufactured from the metals so produced, giving employment in turn to several million additional persons. If you accept a broad description, we are talking about half the wage-paying jobs in the nation.

Ironworking began, in the United States, back in colonial times, long before credit unions were heard of. The first iron works was probably built near Lynn, Massachusetts, in 1646. It was almost certainly the first continuing manufacturing establishment in the American colonies. Some say there was an earlier attempt to start an iron business near Jamestown, Virginia, in 1622, but that the entire crew was massacred by Indians on the first day they went out to fire the furnace. Even so, it was in Massachusetts where U.S. ironmaking got its first successful start. If you visit Lynn, the same town where credit union crusader Roy Bergengren grew up in later years, they will show you this iron works, restored by the local historical society, and still standing on the bank of the Saugus River.

After the original start at Lynn, iron works began springing up all over the colonies. Typically they were small, individual enterprises serving local needs, seldom employing as many as a dozen men. They made a few implements out of cast iron, which was hard metal, but too brittle to be hammered or forged. They also made bar iron, which because it contained less carbon could be pounded or forged into tools, nails, horseshoes, hinges, and wagon tires. The bar iron was not only supplied to blacksmiths and gunsmiths, but also, in the short lengths called "merchant bars," to peddlers who sold the iron from door to door. Householders bought it to fashion their own hardware. Some families, in fact, made nails at home during the winter to supplement the family income; strips of bar iron were locked in a special vise and banged with a hammer to form the nailhead and point. It paid well for a man who could make 2,000 nails a day, for nails were precious; there are reports that when families moved, they sometimes burned down the old house to recover the valuable nails for the new one.

By 1750, the total production of the American colonies was challenging the proud output of England and Wales.

British industrialists were complaining bitterly that the colonies, by making their own iron and iron products, were depriving them of the legitimate market which all colonies were supposed to provide. So in 1750 Parliament enacted a law forbidding the colonies to construct any additional iron-making facilities beyond those already in operation. Not surprisingly, the American iron industry swung behind the revolutionary cause. There are some interesting footnotes to history here. No less than six signers of the Declaration of Independence were dependent for part of their income on iron works. Ethan Allen was an ironworker during several years of his earlier life in Connecticut. George Washington's father was an owner of the Principio Company, the largest of the colonial iron producers. When the fighting began, although most colonial foundries were too small to produce the heavy ordnance needed for warfare, there were already plants in Connecticut and New Jersey grown large enough to cast and finish the cannon needed by the Continental armies.

Yet it was not until after the Civil War that the industry changed in any significant fashion. For an entire century it had continued to grow in much the same pattern —still pinned close to the market centers by inadequate transportation, and still producing the same too-brittle cast iron and too-soft wrought iron, both unsuited to the new and punishing demands of an expanding frontier. Railroads had to run on stronger, tougher metal than these. Finally came the two discoveries which made possible the almost explosive industrial growth which followed.

The first of these was the discovery of the fantastic iron ore deposits near Lake Superior and the Canadian border. A government surveyor stumbled upon them in 1844. When the Soo Canal was completed in 1885, the ore began to flow through the Great Lakes from mines in Northern Michigan and then Minnesota, shipped to processing plants which became concentrated in the areas surrounding Pittsburgh and Chicago. These rich deposits of ore have been the most productive in the history of the world, providing more than 85 per cent of the iron ore consumed by the United States. Without Lake Superior ore—and the handy water transportation which enabled it to travel 1,000 miles or more at low cost to its market—the United States might not have become the world's leading industrial nation.

The second discovery was the new and cheap process for making steel, called the Bessemer Process. It is named for Sir Henry Bessemer, who patented the process in Great Britain in 1856, but there is evidence that as early as 1847 one William Kelly of Eddyville, Kentucky, had shown how air could be blown through molten iron to burn away excess carbon and other impurities. The first Bessemer steel was made in the U.S. in 1864, and it came as a godsend. It provided the cheap, strong steel needed for the railroads and the bridges and the machines and the buildings of an economy ready to burst its traditional seams. America was built with the steel that poured out of its Bessemer converters, along with the improved furnaces which followed.

Now came the changes that turned ironworking into Big Steel, beginning when Carnegie built the first large

Bessemer plant. Pouring steel at the volume now required was no job for the homemade furnaces on the hillside, inherited from colonial days, but for monster furnaces that could fill the sky with flame. The changes in manufacture grew greater with each new method of handling steel. Today the steel man can shape steel into I-beams, or draw it into wire, or roll it down to the thickness of paper. By endless experiment, and by turning the laboratory microscope on the structure of steel, the steelmaker has learned how—with an infinite variety and combination of alloying metals, heat treatments, and rolling mills—to pour a steel that will stand up under the most awesome conditions of heat or corrosion or stress. And the enormous plant, big as some of the city suburbs where the steelworkers live, produces steel with such accuracy and efficiency that it still costs only a fraction of the price of an equivalent amount of non-ferrous metal. The industry figures it takes something like $100,000 of investment in buildings and equipment today for each man who works in the plant. There are only half a dozen great steel companies, along with quite a number of smaller ones. But even in the so-called small plants, it is a country mile from the gate back to the dim and lofty shed where they pour the steel.

"Our operation is one of those small ones," explains Elmer Zumm, who runs the credit union for 3,600 members at Acme Steel. Acme Steel Corporation is located in Riverdale, out on the industrial prairies which lie south of Chicago. Concrete streets run for miles out here between fields of waving weeds which separate one sprawling and bustling manufacturing island from the next.

Overhead, the high voltage wires run in long, sagging leaps from tower to tower in every direction, and the street is chopped into irregular lengths by the endless switch lines of the nation's railroad center. The Acme plant itself is an L-shaped collection of long and narrow buildings, built on a dozen acres of land jutting out into a bend of the Calumet River. Trains chug past all day, down the tracks between the office building and the main gate. The plant produces hot and cold rolled carbon steel strip, along with such specialty items as steel strapping and strapping tools.

Acme's steelmaking facilities are noteworthy because they employ a steelmaking process new to America. Continuous hot blast cupolas, eight stories high, supply molten metal to top-blown basic oxygen furnaces. The metal comes flowing down the troughs from the cupolas in two endless and blinding streams, spilling into mixers at the bottom. From here, the molten iron is "tapped" into giant ladles which carry it, 75 tons at a time, up to the top of the oxygen converters, which tilt forward like oversize bottles to receive it. The steel is made by shoving a long pipe, or "lance," into the top of the converter, where it blows pure oxygen over the hot metal for 20 minutes, heating it to 3,000° F. Within 40 minutes, the converter tilts backward to pour off the slag and 70 tons of steel.

This is breathtaking speed, as steelmaking goes. The standard open hearth method of most steel plants can produce upwards of 300 tons of steel at a time, but it takes eight to ten hours. By comparison, Acme's cupola-oxygen furnace method makes 70 tons in 40 minutes.

This process ideally suits Acme's chosen role as a smaller, but enterprising and pioneering producer. A great many varieties and grades of steel can be made in a single day. Even before they finish pouring one "heat" of molten steel into ingot molds, over in the teeming aisle, a new and different batch can be charged into the converter.

There are unforgettable sights in a steel mill. One is the pouring of liquid steel into the molds, a white and vicious-looking stream that hurts your eyes. The steel in the molds erupts with a shower of sparks when stirred to break the cooling crust. And when the stripped ingots go past—six feet long and 6 tons in weight—on their way to the "soaking pits" (reheating furnaces) and the blooming mill, they are still red-hot. They can burn your face from 20 feet away.

In the blooming mill, which looks like the biggest washday wringer in the world, the ingots are shaped into slabs and billets for all the manufacturing operations which follow. The glowing red ingots slam into the rollers and crunch back and forth 20 times, while the operator plays his levers like piano keys, flipping the slabs over, narrowing them, and rolling them out in an ever-lengthening strip to the required thickness. In the workingman's aristocracy of the steel plant, the blooming mill operator ranks about as high as they come. He is paid to know exactly how much squeeze to put on every kind of steel, and how much screwdown to apply for each pass through the rolls, before he sends the slab down the roller bed to the billet mills, and to the swinging saws which cut them into 30-foot lengths in a grandest display of flying sparks.

Another spectacular sight is at the end of the hot strip mills, where the steel strip comes whipping out of the finishing stands at speeds above 1,200 feet per minute, hissing and bouncing in rippling folds like a 150-foot red snake down the runout table, until it whams into the coiler. The fellows who watch the dials and flip the levers to control the accelerated speed of the lengthening strip from one roller to the next are more of the plant's working aristocracy. Some wear business suits and white shirts, along with their hard hats.

Leaning back in his chair in the office, credit union treasurer Elmer Zumm explains, "Most people don't realize it, but practically all steel is made to order these days. There are so many different kinds of steel and so many ways it can be finished, even in a plant this size, that there's no way to stockpile it. It has become a precise and accurate business. That new melt shop and blooming mill on the back lot cost the company something like $35,000,000. It takes brains to handle that much equipment and make it pay." When he first started working in Acme's payroll department back in 1927, Elmer concedes, the hiring office still took a good look at the size of a steelworker's muscles; before those hydraulic levers were installed, they used to turn the rollers down with big hand wheels. Today they are just as likely to give an applicant an aptitude test and ask for his high school diploma.

What is a steelworker like? Is he the storybook version of a broad-shouldered giant from Middle Europe, six feet tall and speaking broken English? Well, at Acme, the steelworkers are mostly guys named Smith and Johnson and Murphy, who drive to work from all over the Chicago area. Some drive from towns over in Indiana, 40 miles or more away. Of course, the fellow pushing a broom in the No. 4 Mill may also be a transient, working a few months here before he moves on. But as a small, economy-sized steel works, Acme is not plagued as much with such problems as big steel mills, where labor turnover may reach 25 per cent in a single year. Acme's seniority list is impressive. Employees generally stay with their jobs and raise their kids on the pay checks they bring home.

"We've got plenty of smart ones, but we've got some real knuckle-heads, too," Elmer Zumm confides. "I guess we'll always get our share of them in a steel mill." Even if you forget the transients and drifters, there are more than enough steady employees who can be talked into buying any shiny article of trade a fast-thinking salesman pushes at them. Garnishments pop up every month in the personnel office, although they are fewer than they used to be, and the credit union is everlastingly bailing out of trouble somebody who should have known better. Elmer averages an hour or two every day on the telephone. Even so, things are far better than they once were.

When the credit union was started in 1937, with 15 members and $75, the plant employed about 1,200 people. The effects of the depression were still haunting memories. Steel workers had worked 11 and 13 hour shifts during those times, and were glad to have the jobs, because many employees were only working on alternate weeks. Everybody worked on straight time. There was no overtime, no paid vacations. The only fringe benefit anybody can remember was Workmen's Compensation. It was 1932 when the eight-hour day came in with Roosevelt and the Blue Eagle. It was in 1941, when the war started, that the plant first began operating around the clock and needed more help than it could get.

Since he became treasurer of the Acme Steel Credit Union in 1942, Elmer Zumm has seen all the ups and downs from the working side of the desk. He is a quiet one, a thin soft-spoken spectacled man who usually looks more worried than he is. The girls in the office have seldom seen him excited, unless you count the times when he caught somebody trying to cheat one of his members. When Elmer took over as part-time treasurer in 1942, in addition to his regular job in the company payroll department, the credit union had grown in five years to 1,800 members and about $250,000 of assets. By the time he became the full time manager in 1956, the credit union had grown to 3,250 members and $2,300,000 in assets. The original office was a little building next to the loading dock. Big trucks pulled in and out all day long, blocking the doorway, filling the place with exhaust fumes, and generating so much internal combustion uproar that at times nobody could work. But what Elmer Zumm remembers most vividly was the time an overhead crane operator swung a few tons of steel too far at the end of his hook, and punched a hole through the wall of the office. "It threw bricks all over the credit union," he recalls.

The credit union didn't shut down then, and it hasn't shut down since. In the late '50's, when the steelworkers' union was out for four months on strike, Elmer hurried to the labor union officers and to top management and got them both to agree they should pass anybody through the gate who wanted to go to the credit union. The credit union stayed open. Service was not cut back in any way, not even the loan service. Borrowers were told if they would meet their interest payments, they could forget about payments on the principal until the strike was over. Otherwise, it was business as usual. The word got around fast at the union hall, and the wives talked about it on the telephone. "The good will we created was tremendous," Elmer recalls. "I'll bet we picked up 200 new members as soon as they went back to work."

"Funny thing, too," he adds. "We thought we would get lots of large withdrawals, and lots of requests for big loans. But we didn't. They left their money in the credit union, and the loan applications we got were just for emergencies. It came as a real surprise to me, and it taught me plenty about the way people think when they work for a living in an industrial plant. We have had other strikes since then, not to mention a couple of business recessions when there were layoffs, and the pattern is always the same. When the plant is busy and everything looks hunkydory, *both* our shares and our loans go up. But when the work slows down for any reason, *both* the shares and the loan demand slow down, too. Interesting, huh?

"We'll always have slow periods, even without strikes, because they are built into the steel business. Those fluctuations in the industry which get written up in the *Wall Street Journal,* they come about partly because the steel industry is a seasonal business, like anti-freeze or swimming suits. Ever think of that? Business gets good for steel plants when the builders start putting up buildings in the spring, or when the auto plants start tooling up a new model, or what have you. We feel it here at Acme, just like everybody else. Remember what I said about steel being made to order? We wait until the orders come in before we can make the steel, and that means that things are going to get slow around here a couple of months, maybe, out of every year. We have to run the credit union to anticipate such times."

Heading into its 25th anniversary year, the Acme Steel Credit Union has pushed its share total up to $4,000,000, mostly with the help of what Elmer Zumm calls "The System." When a loan is approved, Elmer reaches for a pencil, and says, "Look here, Joe, your first month's payment on that loan comes to $68, including the interest and the payment on the principal. Let's just round that off to a monthly payment of $70, and put the difference into shares—OK?" Elmer hardly ever mentions the fact that Acme Steel Credit Union uses a straight principal-and-interest method, charging a flat one per cent on the unpaid balance, so the actual amount due becomes a little less each succeeding month. Because that's how "The System" works: each borrower must save at least a dollar the first month, and if it turns out to be quite a bit more each month before the loan is paid off, so much the better. Out of 3,600 members, an average of 1,800 are borrowers. The way Elmer sees it, the credit union should get at least a dollar a month from every saver and every borrower. The average loan balance is about $1,500, almost twice the average you'll find in nearby credit unions. At the same time, the average share balance is $950, an astronomical sum which never fails to astonish these same credit unions. If they ask how he does it, Elmer Zumm answers with the same disarming directness which got him elected, at various times, as the president of his local chapter and of the Illinois Credit Union League. He says there is no magical charm brewed in the white-hot oxygen furnaces at Acme Steel, which somehow makes it easy for steelworkers to save. "Phooey," he says. "All credit unions could do what we do, if they tried something like our 'System' to bring the money in. And they could also set up their office hours like we do, so anybody on any of the three shifts can get to the credit union office three times a week. No shift worker has to come back from Indiana to talk to the Acme Steel Credit Union."

Like everybody else connected with the steel business, Zumm realizes that there may be serious tests ahead. Geologists warn that the still huge Lake Superior deposits of high-grade ore, if mined at present rates, may be worked out by the year 1975 or, at latest, 2000. It may happen in our lifetime. Much depends, meanwhile, on experiments to develop commercially successful processes for utilizing lower grade ores, particularly the ore called *taconite,* which is found in deposits measured in billions of tons in the same region at the head of the Great Lakes. Taconite is a rock so hard it cannot be drilled with any ordinary equipment. It contains only 20 to 30 per cent iron, a mixture far too lean for present steel furnaces. These handicaps are being met today by a procedure which begins with "jet piercing" the ore instead of drilling, using jets of flame to chip out the blasting holes. The ore is ground to a powder, from which the iron concentrate is first extracted with magnets, then mixed with water to form mud balls, or pellets, containing 60 to 65 per cent iron. Pellets make wonderful furnace feed. But few believe the steel industry's problems have been solved by these achievements. The taconite process works, but it is formidably expensive; the plants cost millions. Production cannot be stepped up in an emergency, as mining could be. Many say that the taconite process, no matter how it is improved, can never replace the working of soft ores. Time will tell. The final result will surely affect every member of the Acme Steel Credit Union, all others employed in the industry, and every citizen of North America.

New challenges are coming, too, from other metals, especially aluminum. To be sure, there are plastics and laminated woods as strong as steel, and these have their importance. But so far, the biggest inroads on the traditional territories staked out by steel appear to be coming from aluminum, a metal weighing only one-third as much as iron, yet one which has nearly as many applications. Aluminum can be alloyed, cast, rolled, formed, and drawn. It is being used for engine blocks, airplane wings, electric cables, auto grilles, and household siding. It doesn't rust. Many of aluminum's markets have clearly come at the expense of the steel industry and its problems.

Aluminum is the most abundant metal on earth, a chemical component of common clay, and of practically every rock except sandstone and limestone. Yet up to 75 years ago aluminum ranked as a prohibitively priced metal, not too far removed in cost from the ruby and sapphire which are the gem forms of its oxide ore. It was only in 1886, when Charles Hall of the U.S. and the Frenchman Heroult simultaneously discovered a relatively inexpensive way to derive metallic aluminum from the oxide through electrolysis. Now the oxide is melted in solution in a carbon-lined tank, which serves as a cathode, and carbon anodes are then plunged into this "pot" by an overhead bus bar. The electric current separates the oxide into metallic aluminum, which sinks to the bottom of the tank, and into oxygen, which gradually burns up the anodes. The main requirement for the process is plenty of electricity, since it takes up to 12 kilowatt hours of electricity to make a pound of aluminum. This explains why aluminum reduction plants are so often located near hydroelectric power, even though they may be many miles from the nearest source of bauxite, the basic ore. The aluminum "pigs" are shipped directly to the processing plants.

One of these processing plants is the monster Reynolds plant in McCook, Illinois, located so close to Acme Steel that the credit union treasurers can easily meet for lunch. Reynolds-McCook is a sheet mill, the largest processing unit in the Reynolds industrial combine. Company literature says it is the biggest factory under one roof in the world. Here they roll aluminum sheet and plate (anything above .250 inch is plate, and anything below .008 inch is foil), and aluminum coils. The plant has turned out a million pounds of this aluminum sheet in a single day.

There are some noticeable differences between the processing of aluminum and steel. Aluminum pigs are melted down with alloying elements in the furnaces, at a lower temperature than steel, and then poured by the D-C casters into huge mattress-shaped ingots, which can be made to weigh anywhere from 3,600 to 15,000 pounds. These big ingots have to be "scalped" to remove their rough surface crust, and then "soaked" in a furnace to bring their temperature back up to the 900° required for the trip through the "hot line," where the metal is rolled into strips a half-inch thick and a quarter of a mile long. After this, it may be heat-treated and cold-rolled, then slit or chopped up into sheets. These operations, like steel, have their spectacular points. In the credit union office they talk with real respect about the big tapering mill. Part of its base, they say, is the largest poured casting in the world; it was cast in Germany, in 1955, and arrived at the plant on two flat cars after two months of travel over a special route worked out by the U.S. Navy. This mill can roll a sheet of aluminum tapered from 1/10,000 of an inch on one edge, up to 1½ inch on the other, if such variants are required, but despite such differences, the processing of aluminum is not unlike the processing of steel. The people who do it for a living are much the same. They belong, in fact, to the steelworkers' union.

Most of them belong, too, to a remarkably successful credit union. As credit unions go, the Reynolds-McCook Credit Union is brand new, but already it provides a convincing demonstration of how fast credit unions can benefit people working in big industry. There is a long-standing company policy at McCook that if any worker has creditors who process as many as three wage assignments or garnishments with the company, he will be discharged. Prior to 1959, this policy had led to a long series of differences between the labor union and company management. The man who recognized that a credit union would be the solution to this sticky situation was Bob Pryor, president of Local 3911 of the United Steel Workers, who is now the loan officer of the credit union. Pryor had been a credit union member in a previous job and knew what he was talking about. He was backed up by the plant manager, who was much concerned when he saw the number of credit complaints received by the personnel department increasing rather than diminishing, despite the company's rather grim stand, so the credit union was established in 1959, with approval on all sides.

The first need, Treasurer Howard Holubetz confides, was that of "getting our people out of hock, and keeping them out." Setting up shop in a tiny abandoned guard house near the main gate, the credit union began making job-saving loans of $25 to $100, gradually moving up to an average $500 as the share capital rolled in. Within two years, the credit union had 1,600 members and a half million in assets. Impressed by what it saw, the company provided better office space for the credit union next to the plant cafeteria, even including an anteroom for interviewing.

In the beginning there were two distinct types of in-hock members. Charlie Jones, for example, was accident prone in terms of installment buying and loan shark relations. From the time he left a one-mule tenant farm down in Arkansas and moved north into a realm where it is customary to pay cash wages for hard work, Charlie was resolved to support his family better and to live better himself.

In considerable part, he succeeded. But during his first five years with Reynolds, the Jones family's needs kept getting ahead of the breadwinner's paychecks. Charlie is a natural born bill-payer, but fast-talking sales people found this out, and united in selling Charlie everything that could be provided for a dollar down and the rest continuously—from electric blankets to a tube-lighted tombstone on the layaway plan. When Jones' available cash ran out, the loan sharks strolled in. Charlie recognized that the interest rates were coming high, and that ten per cent monthly was a shade on the steep side. But he didn't think too much about it. "When I share-cropped cotton back in Arkansas," Charlie explains, "the landlord cheated me out of that much, twice over."

Charlie's wage check grew, but the cash demands of loan sharks and installment collectors grew much faster. Then came the day when one of them "garnishayed" Charlie's wages. Before the month was over, another writ of attachment was served against Charlie's payroll credit. This time the crew foreman patted Charlie's strong right arm, and said, "Look, Jonesy, company rules say if you get one more garnishment, you're through." Painstaking workman that he normally is, Charlie Jones flinched so violently that he almost stripped a brand new set of trimmer gears. Then he told the foreman that he owed at least three other past-due accounts, any one of which could bring down the fatal papers.

The foreman hurried to a phone and arranged a talk with the new credit union. He and Charlie checked out long enough for Charlie to explain his dilemma to the credit committee. The treasurer sat in on the discussion. By the time it was over, Charlie joined the credit union, authorized a $40 monthly payroll deduction for shares, and received an immediate loan to cover all his imperiling debts, totaling $380. One year later, debt-free and owner of $480 in shares, Charlie was willing to tell anybody, "This is the only really good job I ever had—and that credit union sure saved it for me."

In like manner and despite its extreme youth, the Reynolds-McCook Credit Union has saved dozens of jobs. President Maceo Liddell estimates no fewer than a hundred. "This is just one of a tubfull of good deeds we manage to get done. But speaking as a guy who puts in up to forty free hours a week for this credit union, I'd say that saving just one job is worth the price of admission." Treasurer Howard Holubetz, who comes into the office mornings after working a full noon-to-eight shift in the plant, nods agreement.

For a different viewpoint, take member Tom Lamont. Tom's job was never imperiled. Tom is a wounded Marine veteran drawing a $200 major disability stipend every month, but this doesn't prevent his earning $400 as a fireman at Reynolds-McCook. His wife earns an additional $350 a month as a products inspector. The Lamonts are a hard-working, sure-earning couple, yet until quite recently, they just weren't the saving kind. Tom can't explain why; he only knows that by the end of the year he had never stashed away as much as a dime—never, that is, until the credit union came along. The Lamonts joined up at the first meeting. After 16 months, the couple had shareholdings totaling $3,200, enough to pay an extra week's wages in dividends.

Tom says now, "The way I see it, I'm a fairly average American worker, nothing special, although I'd estimate that my wife is special. I never had any grudge against saving, but no message about saving ever really got through to me. But the credit union at this plant, that's what did it. I know most of the guys who started it. I know some of the people who got credit union loans, and I heard them tell how much the loans meant—paying for sickness, sending the kids to school, getting loan sharks off their backs, and so on. This credit union is a personal thing for all the 2,000 people who work in this plant. But what finally sold me was that all the officers, directors, and committeemen work for free and on their own time—just because they believe in credit unions. How do you like that? So my wife and I figured we better put our money in, and now we're going places with what we earn. A credit union takes you places. . . ."

Reynolds-McCook Credit Union, from all indications, will be taking them places for a long time to come. Both the labor union and company management are represented on the board of directors, which democratically includes two from the cast house, one from the hot line, two from shipping, two from inspection, one from finishing, one from heat-treat, and one from top management. Two are foremen, and seven are hourly employees. George Staunton, company training coordinator, is chairman of the credit committee. There is no friction whatsoever. "We keep labor union business and company business out of credit union business," says president Liddell, "and everybody stays happy."

There are other encouraging signs, too, for the members of this credit union. Reynolds, which prides itself on being an innovator, is moving not only into new methods of shaping and embossing aluminum, but also into new methods, some of them still top secret, for coating and painting their prime metal which hold much promise for the future. Soon, they hope, there may be new products made from aluminum which are now customarily made from wood, or cement, or steel, or glass, moving into acceptance in the same way as the aluminum boats and furniture and building materials which not long ago surprised the world. If so, the Reynolds-McCook Credit Union will certainly continue to prosper. It has done much to contribute to the stability and the morale of the working force at the great plant it serves. Like thousands of other industrial firms which receive such unasked benefits, the parent company will be glad to see this credit union grow, taking its growth as evidence of the increasing capacity of all its employees to manage their own financial affairs with competence in a challenging and changing world.

# [ 6

# *Credit Unions and the Community Spirit*

One of the rewarding phases of learning about credit unions is the rediscovery of the American community. By basic definition a community is a body of people living under the same general conditions. The same broad designation is apropos of most memberships of most credit unions, whatever the specific classification, i.e., industrial, church, teachers, government workers, or whatever.

In the United States less than three per cent of all duly chartered credit unions are classified as community; the phrase "duly chartered" is used because in most instances the classification is a term or a stipulation of charter. But implicitly, even if in varying degrees, any credit union is a community enterprise. In Canada close to 40 per cent of all credit unions are formally listed as "communities" and similar or higher proportions hold in many of the new frontiers of credit unions. It follows that contemporary credit unions in the United States which function on a residential or prescribed area basis are especially revealing to any student of credit and especially revealing to those who would learn of credit by helping create it in community with others.

This, of course, is an instance of history repeating itself. As we have already noticed, the original credit societies as conceived and materialized in nineteenth century Germany by Raiffeisen were preponderantly residential or community. So was Desjardins' original American credit union as founded at Levis, Quebec, in 1900. So in living, thriving reality is the Hereford Federal Credit Union of Deaf Smith County, Texas.

Deaf Smith County, Texas, is big. It covers 1,507 square miles and includes the sizable town of Hereford, named for the famous beef cattle breed, and it is the home of a community credit union, the Hereford Texas Federal which is authorized to serve the entire county plus all citizens within a 25-mile radius of Hereford town.

The community services which this symbolic credit union performs range from helping a gifted youngster through high school to founding a self-perpetuating village.

This latter story is one of the unusual entries in the saga of credit unions. During the past century which has seen the United States changed from more than one-half to less than one-eighth agrarian, thousands of country villages and rural crossroads have been permitted to burn, wait vacant, rot, collapse or otherwise fade away. In some part this chronicle of abandonment is inevitable. In great part it is deplorable both for country living and practical farming—specific enterprises requiring specific goods. This is true in every state and particularly true in Texas.

Ten miles or a Texas rock-throw southwest of Hereford is a farming and ranching community called Easter. In earlier times Easter had its own school, its own stores, and other trade facilities. By 1958 only its cotton gin and grain elevator remained active. Otherwise Easter was just another dying crossroad. When there was instant need for a loaf of bread, or when Junior got sick, or when the three-quarter inch bolt on the gang plow assembly broke (and the tool kit held only half-inch bolts) somebody had to drop his work, hop into the family car, and make the twenty-mile round trip to town.

During 1958 a German-descended farmer of the neighborhood decided to take a bold step toward remedying the situation. As a long time and long proved credit union borrower and shareholder, the farmer headed for Hereford and the attractive credit union building. There he outlined his idea to Mrs. Dyalthia Benson, the combination philosopher, nursemaid, and manager of the Hereford Federal Credit Union. The farmer stated his case and received a loan which enabled him to refurbish a fertilizer business in the area of Easter village. The enterprise not only succeeded but serves to remind local customers of the advantages of nearness to necessary supplies.

So the farmer went back to the credit union, and with unanimous approval of the credit committee, received a loan of $8,000. He used the money to buy fertilizer tanks from the chemical company, for installing a gasoline pump, building a storehouse with 1,000 square feet of floor space, purchasing the basic fixtures and installing a nucleus of stock for a new store.

From the first he found his country neighbors appreciative of the time saving and convenience of having a shopping center within easy reach. As soon as the new market at Easter crossroads was ready for business, bakeries and dairies in Hereford and farther towns of the area gladly provided daily deliveries of bread and milk to the reawakened village. A wholesale grocery firm in Amarillo, the nearest city, agreed to provide on consignment a line of staple food items for shelf and bin stock.

Hardware, too, is a key necessity of country living and work; for practical farming, repair hardware is almost as indispensable as seeds. At best the costs are formidable. A mere line of bolts suitably sized for repairing basic farm machinery costs at least $600. But the community's year-around costs of making hurried trips to distant towns in order to procure it, comes vastly higher. So much of the $8,000 loan went for hardware.

Treasurer-manager Dyalthia Benson summarizes: "Our member has benefitted by the business loan and the credit union is really appreciated for establishing the Easter Community Stores which serve the local farmers so very helpfully."

The credit union's resurrection of Easter village is also a reminder of the special and enduring, even if underestimated, importance of farm earnings. And a visible reminder that American enterprise still rises from the good earth. Though actual farm income has dwindled to a bare tenth of the total national earning, that tenth stays the dynamic minority. If anyone doubts this, let him query the Ford Motor Company, which still earns a very substantial part of its net profits from farm tractors and accompanying machinery. Or ask the chemical companies which profit most surely from fulfilling needs of a great new era of soil enrichers and improvers. Or the big petroleum companies which profit not so much from gasoline or heating oils as from the many salable byproducts of petroleum, including pesticides, fertilizers, weed killers and hundreds more which find their decisive markets on farms, orchards and ranges. Not that the town doesn't participate, too. The Hereford Texas Federal Credit Union has undertaken at least 13,000 other successful ventures in helping members help themselves since the credit union began.

Times were hard when it was founded; 1934 was perhaps the darkest of all the depression years for Texas. Dyalthia Benson early developed the practice of visiting local earners on pay day to set forth the merits of credit union participation. It took a lot of time, work and shoe leather, but as one who devotedly believes in credit unions, Mrs. Benson considered the missions of mutual benefit. One such citizen was a soda fountain boy who joined at the age of 17 in 1937, saving dimes while going to high school. The credit union has since provided him with the money to get married, to furnish his home, to pay for autos and vacations, to start a restaurant business, and finally to open a profitable "cage egg" business on the side. All told, Bill Brown has received and repaid 18 credit union loans totaling $13,775.50 since 1937, and his pass book currently shows a share balance over $1,000. His wife and three children are also members. Only the name is fictitious in this story.

Today Bill Brown owns an attractive home and a good business, is head of a lovely family, and a respected community leader. He has proved equal competence with his credit union, which he has served for a dozen years as a key committee member and director. One after another he has encouraged employees and business associates to join the fold. In 1958 Bill volunteered as co-signer of a loan of $4,000 which enabled his brother-in-law to establish a new filling station. It is proving successful. At Brown's suggestion his father-in-law, a normally self-sufficient farmer, came to the Hereford Credit Union for a five-digit operational loan which earned its own repayment within three years. Bill's father-in-law also came to the credit union for a readily granted loan with which to meet large and protracted medical expenses. A few years ago when Bill's mother's home burned, another valid credit union loan served to restore the homestead and to enhance its value.

As time and needs require, Bill Brown expects to seek, receive and repay many more credit union loans. Mrs. Benson, the treasurer-manager, confirms this, "We expect to continue serving Bill's family, helping to educate his children with loans to supplement their savings already started for that purpose. . . . We are proud of the opportunity that this credit union has had to serve Bill Brown and hundreds of others like him."

Hereford, Texas is a growing town with a workday census of about 8,500. In its true Texas way the place has spread in friendliness. So has the solitary credit union, including its nest, a single-story brick home down on Schley Street. The town is its front yard; the far-flung Deaf Smith County and substantial areas of two adjoining counties are its living "spread." The membership is of all ages, and circumstances—school children, high school and college students, farmers, ranchers, shopkeepers, professional men and women, cattle buyers and brokers, cotton dealers and suppliers, and so on.

The board of directors includes the president, vice-president, two directors, all currently men, and the woman treasurer-manager. The credit committee includes three regular and three alternate members; one of the latter a woman. The supervisory committee is comprised of three men. Seven of the eight-member education committee are men; one is a prominent local minister.

The dividends are compounded semi-annually. A full month's dividend credit is paid on shares deposited during the first five days of each month. The unsecured loan limit is now $750, plus unpledged shares. Loans are now available for terms up to five years. Smaller loans are expedited by the board's appointment of a special loan officer who is authorized to approve unsecured loans of an emergency nature.

Although the credit union's loan lists are almost as long and varied as the Hereford telephone directory, most loans are made on the standard Benson "level payment plan." The designation is self-explanatory. If you borrow $600 for 24 months, you repay in 24 monthly payments of $33 each. This "clears" the note, pays a total of $75 in interest charges and adds $117 to your shares or savings account; no extra charge for loan or savings insurance, no tricky fees or red tape, no abstract or legal papers racket.

An able rival in popularity and personalized benefit is

the "Hereford Special" for students. These are one-year, September to September loans, with a limit of $300 per student per year. They are open and renewable to high school and college students, also to participants in special training courses, business or commercial colleges and all accredited adult education courses. The annual interest is only three per cent: September datings permit the borrowers to apply summer earnings to repayment and renewal.

The sense of the student loans is future building. To date more than a thousand have been granted. Hundreds have supplied young members with educational resources which could not have been attained otherwise. That was the experience of young Joe Jones who managed to scratch through grade school and the first year of high school. At that point he was obliged to drop out of school and take a full time job.

But Joe refused to quit his schooling. A devoted credit union member, he came to Miss Dyalthia and laid his cards on her table and the credit committee's. As a result he was granted the standard student loan of $300 at three per cent. He used the money to take extension courses for after-hour study, persevered until he had won credits sufficient for graduation. When Joe learned that he would be permited to be graduated "in person" with the class he had kept up with, he remembered to mail an invitation to the staff of the Hereford Credit Union. At curtain raising time there was the entire office staff in the audience. Thus are life long and life loyal members made.

Though its members range from less than a year old

to well over 80, the Hereford Credit Union makes a devoted play to interest the young, in the belief that thrift habits and credit building are best begun early. Children are particularly welcome and however busy or long the day (office hours are 8:30 to 5:00 on week days and 9 to 12 on Saturdays) the office staff always has time for young folk, whether toddlers or teen-agers. Dime and quarter savings cards are provided without cost for the convenience and advancement of very young customers. Attractive coin banks are sold at cost. A wall motto counsels "Credit Union Is a Family Affair."

As a community or residential credit union, Hereford Texas Federal Credit Union knows it must live by neighborliness. It must progress without the convenient and not always recommendable crutch of pay roll deductions, or the rectitude factors incident to *not* "letting down the people at the shop," or the persuasions which apply to congregation, club, or fraternity members. Motivations for membership are necessarily variable. Its community ties must be revisable and extendable.

As Alf Dugal puts it, "When people stop needing credit unions, there won't be much need for anything else." Alf Dugal is an untiring flock tender for a community credit union in Maine–Ste. Famille's Parish at Lewiston. He has spent his best years at learning the job and in helping others learn it. In the process he has received and cherished a great deal of help. Givers include Monsignor Nonorgues, a veteran pastor of the parish, which some have described as "a French-speaking island in an ocean of Maine accents."

The community began as a weavers' colony. During

recent years cotton has gone South, woolens have gone down, and many of the parishioners have been able to go ahead only with very considerable difficulties. All these facts of contemporary life have stressed the enduring truth that in any free enterprise society the saving and good use of money, including the development of credit, is a basic phase of enlightened schooling.

Among the believers in the foregoing is Sister Marie Bernard, principal of the Holy Family Parochial School of the Sainte Famille Parish. Another is Father Nonorgues. Through the years his privilege of good works has included overcoming the argument that a community which is short of money has a rather dim chance for going long on thrift. But Monsignor Nonorgues contends that a poor parish with an ingrown determination to remain self-sufficient and solvent is the best possible vineyard for the fruits of thrift. This conviction is more than casual philosophy. It is the practical tenet of a priest who lives a religion of the blood, flesh and guts as well as the immortal soul of man.

A third of a century ago when the Monsignor came to the parish as a temporary vicar the fabrics industries were beginning to descend into rough waters. Waters grew much deeper and rougher as the depression settled. The then young priest faced the problem of protecting his flock from what he terms "economic slaughter" by loan sharks. He moved boldly to help found a parish credit union which now has share assets well over $1,000,000, with more than $330,000 already returned in dividends to parish members who are the shareholders.

Ste. Famille's Parish Credit Union never was much of

a display group. Most of the time since 1938 when Parishioner Alfred Dugal took over as full time and for many years unpaid treasurer, the credit union's headquarters was an otherwise unused garage in Dugal's home. There is now an adequate but modest headquarters building, and Alf Dugal remains the one-man staff. Four other parish credit unions now thrive and grow in the same area. Local bankers who used to rue the "shuttle-throwing Frenchies who speak no English except 'Please lend me' " are now relieved of concern. The shuttle-throwers now have their own credit facilities, as valuable to the community as any of the banks.

In 1955 Sister Marie and her faculty of the Holy Family School decided to teach thrift instead of merely delivering an annual talk about it. As a first step in planning, the Sisters decided to write down a statement of goals and an objective analysis of what the school had to gain, or better say give, from teaching thrift practice. The first rough draft was approximately this:

"The goals are: (1) To help our pupils appreciate the values and good uses of money; (2) To correlate and connect thrift teaching with practical teaching of arithmetic; (3) To learn the civic and community values of saving and to understand the differences between ethical lending and borrowing practices and loan shark operations; (4) To help our children personally develop systematic saving habits. . . ."

As usual the goals were easier to state than to attain. Since most of the parish families are of low income brackets, weekly or interval savings would necessarily be small by averages. As their parents have learned before them, now the children would have to understand that the essential merits of thrift are qualitative rather than quantitative, and that consistency is the best criterion. It would have to be made clear to all that the child who saves a penny or nickle a week from his own earnings deserves as much or more credit as a child who deposits part or even all of his unearned allowance.

Where would the money be placed? Established banks and other commercial institutions in the area have the usual one-dollar minimum deposit rule. It was evident that weekly savings of most pupils would average less than a dollar each, and that teamwork or "school spirit" would be impaired by putting individual banks between the school project and the individual pupils. Further, as a quick checkup showed, the local banks were not especially eager to stand in the middle.

A local bank president summarized glumly: "Those school kid accounts would probably average out between three and four dollars a year apiece. Handling them on an individual basis would cost this bank about the same amount in staff and overhead. Besides, when Pappy goes on a bender and draws out Junior's savings the bank has no choice but to obey parent's signature." Another bank man was openly cynical about the future of the proposed deposits. "The trouble with this kid account stuff is that it maybe starts off with a bang. Then the circus comes, or the state fair opens, or the baseball season starts, or the father loses his job or mother loses hers, and away go Johnny's or Susie's savings."

Sister Marie talked with Alfred Dugal, who has done so much to make the parish credit union tick. Brother

Alfred explained the legal barriers incident to founding a credit union exclusively for children. State and Federal laws require that duly elected officers and directors be adult, as do insurance and bonding requirements. But Alf Dugal, the Monsignor and the credit union directors assembled in Dugal's home garage and voted to invite Sister Marie and her school to form a special Junior Department of the Ste. Famille Parish Credit Union.

The virtually instant acceptance of the offer meant that the credit union was taking on an almost fabulous workload. Every pupil requires an individual pass book which must be posted and balanced weekly. Individual savings deposits are recorded in triplicate, one copy for the saver, one for the school and one for the credit union. But the community gains by the enlightened work to channel the savings of its children into a dynamic credit pool which directly benefited all 1,100 members of the parish credit union and the credit needs of the community at large. Moreover, the credit union stood to gain shares and a far more important asset in good will. The children today are the indispensable members and officers of tomorrow, and even today they influence their parents to align themselves with the established credit union.

The junior credit union came into being with the 1956 school year. Pupils who wished to join filled in a formal application which clearly explained the functions and rules. Explanatory letters were dispatched to all parents. Thursday was designated as Savings Day. Pupils were asked to turn in their savings during a 10-minute monitor period following the usual 8:30 morning convocation. The Thursday noon period is set aside for "check and entry-making" under supervision of the principal and the Sister or Sisters assigned to noon hour duty. A "Savings Monitor" is elected by each of the fifteen classrooms and two outstanding eighth-graders are honored by being appointed supervising monitors.

By the end of the first school year a good majority, about 500 of the then 700 pupils, had joined the junior credit union. The average individual savings were and still are about 26 cents per week per member. By the end of its second year, the junior credit union had assets or shares of about $10,000 and withdrawals were averaging only about five per cent of deposits. The growth pattern continues intact. As this is written nearly 600 of the 745 pupils actively participate in the savings program and approximately two-thirds of the graduates keep up the good work, either in high school or private employment. This year "charter" members of the savings group are using their savings and established credit to help them to colleges and advanced trade or business schools.

Sister Marie notes that, "Filling in and signing their own application cards are important experiences for our youngsters. This is usually the first time they have been asked to sign a document for themselves in their own right. The experience of this signing impresses on the youngster the fact that his share account is his very own. . . ."

All members of the Junior Savings Program receive the prevailing dividend payments of the credit union. This is currently three per cent net plus funds for annual "incentive prizes" of $2 each for the 15 classrooms. Any youngster who makes savings deposits each week for any six months of the school year is eligible. Five of the current prizes were won by pupils with weekly savings averaging less than five cents; as always the accent is on regularity rather than amounts of savings. Even so, the total shares or assets of the junior program keep increasing at the fairly steady rate of about $5,000 per school year while membership slowly but surely approaches the enrollment total.

Sister Marie summarizes: "As expected, the greatest dividends of our savings program are human. It helps our youngsters gain a real appreciation of money, encourages them to develop regular savings habits, shows them the great living importance of arithmetic and helps them understand a number of basic economic problems.

"But by final count the greatest value is to the classroom collectors, the collection supervisors, and the other children who do the bulk of the work. This experience is invaluable. It helps the youngsters gain self-confidence and appreciate their responsibilities to properly attend and respect other people's money. Every week these children handle, count and account for every cent entrusted to them. This gives each the very real satisfaction of usefully sacrificing his own spare time for service to the group. . . ."

Those who learn of credit unions by helping conceive and build them to fit general community needs also learn how to adapt to the special ways and needs of other communities. A roving reporter meets engaging examples. For one, in and around the village of Hesston, Kansas, there is a rural credit union exclusively of and for

Mennonites. This religious brotherhood has tenets of faith which do not permit dealing with any bank or other financial institution owned or kept by persons of other faiths. The approximately 250 Hesston Mennonites have organized and continue to serve and benefit from a credit union which permits them to endure and prosper as wheat and cattle farmers.

Moving westward one meets another community credit union, the Chautauqua of Southwest Kansas, which typifies those developed in a specific place for a specific purpose, in this instance for establishing a rural electric service and enabling members to buy equipment for making effective use of that service.

At Hoisington, Kansas, the Cheyenne Community Credit Union is an impressive resurrection of a one-time railway employee union which was left to perish when the Missouri Pacific closed out a division. The credit union refused to die, reorganized itself as a "country styler," currently is staging a comeback with about $65,000 in assets and 160 loyal members, mostly farmers.

The roots of credit unions keep reaching deeper into American earth. It follows that learning and teaching of credit unions reflects more and more deeply the ever varying American backgrounds. An illustrative and in some part illustrious credit union background is the nation's oldest international farming group. This is the Patrons of Husbandry, or Farmers' Grange; "grange" is Acadian French for "barn," the traditional shaper and prover of farm prosperity or poverty.

Since its eighteenth century beginning in America, the Grange has officially regarded agriculture as a family calling and vocation. Through the years it has kept membership open to all members of farm families, without prejudice of age or sex. It has long been axiomatic that Grange Masters are men, that Grange doers are women, that Grange longevity is rooted in the fact that children members provide an unfailing reservoir of future membership.

This is one vital part of the story of the Grange. Another is that whatever its locale or size the Grange or Patrons of Husbandry remains essentially a study and learning group. Its lecturer or program chairman is one of its most important officers. Free speech and provision of speaking time for men, women and children alike are traditional. Thus through the years and generations all Grange members are encouraged to study together, learn together, in no little part to practice self-expression in open meeting.

From Maine to California and beyond, Grangers, though not always the most prosperous farmers, are traditionally among the more independent and self-expressive. This was true of Connecticut Valley Granges in the lifetimes of Ethan Allen and Cornwallis, and of the then new Pacific Coast Granges at the time Vermont-born Admiral Dewey ordered his combat fleet to weigh anchor from San Francisco harbor and head for Manila Bay.

Fairly recently, and particularly in California, the Farmers' Grange has taken a new mission—that of effectively sponsoring credit unions for the good of its members and their rural neighbors. As this is written, there are 60 Grange-founded credit unions in the United States: 41 of them are in California.

The reason for this is in effective part a Yankee-born,

Boston-raised farm wife, Mrs. Mildred Boyd. Back in January, 1941, Mildred Boyd of Fresno, California, as chairman of the Grange's entertainment committee, invited a speaker to tell the Fresno Grange about credit unions, a then novel subject, at least to the membership of the Fresno Grange. Mildred Boyd was dividing a typically busy day between her housekeeping, her family, their milk cows and her favorite community organization.

As usual the meeting was well attended, with about 125 members on hand. When the lecture was finished, the membership surprised the visiting speaker, as well as Mildred Boyd, by voting to organize its own credit union. Mildred Boyd was no less astonished to hear herself elected treasurer—by acclaim. Almost instantly thereafter she found herself showered with quarters for membership dues. Before the week was finished Mildred Boyd was playing nursemaid for $47 in quarters from 188 brand new members and she was also recipient of a completely bona fide application for a $50 loan. As soon as the charter was granted and officers elected, including Mildred Boyd as regular treasurer, and necessary committees appointed, the loan was granted.

The treasurer now admits that had she ever suspected that her responsibility would presently rise to any vast sum, such as $5,000, she wouldn't have stayed on as treasurer. As her mother had said, "Mildred just never was the money handling kind."

By the end of the first year the Fresno Grange Credit Union's total assets were crowding close to $5,000. But during that same year Mildred Boyd learned that the farm people of her own Grange and neighborhood needed a credit union very badly indeed. Through some 1,000 other Grange members in Fresno County she gathered that credit unions were needed in many other communities. But the infant credit union which met in the parlor of her home (and still does) proved the needs pertinently. Neighbors and fellow Grangers bought shares, but they required larger sums in loans. A first ominous emptiness of the cash box was relieved when an elderly farm neighbor strolled in, joined up, and left $500 in cash for his purchase of shares.

In earlier years Mildred Boyd had known her farming neighbors as open-hearted and cautiously sociable people with deeply ingrained suspicions regarding the intentions of all money lenders. Almost magically the fledgling credit union began changing this. A charter member who was also a first borrower and repayer explained his altered view. "Missus Boyd, you keep this credit union thing in your own home." (She still does.) "I can come into your house with my head high because I know you and all your folks as friendly neighbors. I know I'm welcome in this house. I also know I'm one of the owners of this credit union. So I can come in head up and ask for a loan when I need it. I'm not obliged to come slinking in like at a bank or loan agency."

Mildred Boyd had anticipated this reaction, had deliberately striven to produce it. But her instantly necessary field of learning included intimate, sympathetic understanding of borrowers' needs—for new or used cars, refrigerators, cream separators, seeds, shoes, hospital and medical services and a thousand other items from dentures to dusting planes, and the ever expanding roster of farming needs. Mrs. Boyd knew many of the problems of farm finance at first hand, especially the fact that few farms can be operated wholly on short term credit. Only the minority can make regular monthly interest payments.

In Fresno County approximately 70 per cent of the entire year's farm income is received during the month of December. Inevitably that month of majority intake is crucial to credit management. From December through the planting seasons of April and May, and the subsequent spraying and tending season the neighborly credit union must stand ready with cash or invest briefly in short term Government bonds or similar securities which are instantly convertible to cash. For Autumn harvests are inevitably demanding that cash be spent in order that it may be earned back again. From her own experience, Mildred Boyd recognized the need for using December and nearby pay-off times as an interval for encouraging members to celebrate by buying credit union shares. Her discreet but frank opening question became, "How much of this crop money are you going to be able to help yourself with?"

As she continued to grow into the role of "Mrs. Farmers' Credit Union," with the sympathetic approval and blessings of her husband, Mildred Boyd acquired several convictions which remain steadfast. One is that founding and building countryside credit unions is wholly in keeping with the purpose and ideals of the Grange. Another is that a particular goal of any credit union is that of helping out the younger members, particularly newlyweds who would work together at farming or, indeed, any other worthy trade. Through the years Mildred Boyd has noticed that when the young couple starts out with pre-marriage indebtedness to parents or kin or even a commercial money lender, the premarital obligation poses hazard and problem out of keeping with the actual amount of the indebtedness. Mrs. Boyd believes it is of great importance both economically and psychologically to erase the before-the-marriage debts as quickly and painlessly as possible.

In its first 20 years the Fresno Grange Credit Union has used the discreet championship of young people, including young couples, as a key factor in changing the original $47 in twenty-five cent membership dues to audited assets of more than $1,200,000, with more than $1,000,000 in valid and helpful loans outstanding. Thus far the credit union has lost a grand total of three loans, a loss percentage beginning with a decimal point and four successive zeros.

Personal confidence and neighborly understanding are essential to any competent estimate of credit risk. Accordingly the credit committee of which Mrs. Boyd is a member devotes an average of one hour to every loan application interview.

There have been times when the now most steadfast members of her credit union were "dadburned" if they were going to tell their business or personal problems to any "dadburned woman." In earlier times, Mildred referred the "dadburners" to her late husband, but now it is generally accepted that Mildred Boyd is no female chatterbox or mushhead. She is a farmer as well as a farm wife, a producing partner as well as a skirt wearer. Furthermore, as a long time Granger Mildred had long since learned to recognize and respect the viewpoint of the entire family.

Keeping the Fresno Farmers' Grange credit union headquarters in the treasurer's front parlor has aided this goal enormously. So has the continuing work pattern of neighborliness. The home atmosphere is bona fide and without feminine domination.

Eight of the nine directors are men. All board members and key committeemen meet regularly at least once a month in the Boyd home. By standing invitation and orthodox practice they bring their wives along. The women visit, knit, chat, play bridge or otherwise stay amused in the living room while board meetings proceed in the dining room. The meetings begin promptly at 8:00 P.M., end no later than 10:15. The working quorum is thirteen—directors, officers and members of the supervisors' committee and as occasion requires other committeemen and members. At each meeting one wife takes her turn at "catering"—serving light refreshments for the social hour following the meeting. At least twice yearly, during the Christmas Holidays and following annual election and installation of officers in February, the credit union holds a Pot Luck Supper.

However, the annual meeting, held in January, has now grown too big for any one dwelling. The active membership now stands at 1,489 (of a potential 1,900) and includes about 200 children. Furthermore, visiting Grangers, sometimes 300 to 400, also drop in from out of the night, which in January is usually foggy. Ladies usually "take rotation" at contributing cakes, usually at least a dozen whoppers, sometimes known as "queen sizers," which are auctioned off for purchases of shares in the host credit union. In 1962 the "high cake" brought $900 in share purchases, the donated dozen about $4,000. Originally Mildred Boyd's Yankee conservatism prompted her to predict a $50 share purchase for each cake. But the Grange spirit proved irrepressible. The same spirit now prevails in the regular practice of presenting each baby born to a member or members of the Grange credit union with a $5 share and a prepaid membership.

Mildred Boyd makes yearly visits to Grange groups throughout California to tell the story of credit unions. Like every other community credit union treasurer Mildred Boyd believes in the implicit honesty of the American citizen. She believes that at least nine-tenths of the security or validity of any loan is the personal character of the borrower; the rest is mostly the rational feasibility, or better say, horse sense of the loan as it is granted.

Mildred Boyd sees the gaudy offerings of consumer credit now being waved toward practically everybody as powerful motivation for learning much more about the real meaning of credit. In the countryside of Fresno, California, as in most other American countrysides, offers of credit are now almost as numerous as the three leaves and much more protrusive. Mail order and chain department stores solicit teenage credit buyers of all manner of goods and gadgets, inveigh "small down payment" plus "easy terms" which usually overlook true interest rates, and handily evade the fact that minors are not legally responsible for their incurrence of debt. On the adult side, auto dealers, TV and radio dealers, and appliance firms feature "easy terms," usually without revealing excessive interest rates involved and frequently without openly stating the total indebtedness. The "payment" is $46.19 a month, so who cares how many months or how much of the $46.19 goes specifically for what? Some onlookers view this technique as unmeetable competition. Credit unions see it not as unmeetable competition but rather as reaffirmation of the need to learn what bona fide credit really is; how it can be built and used and perpetuated for the common good.

Far removed from fast-talking salesmen, in the Ranargis settlement, about 60 miles south of Hudson's Bay, line trapper Lol Truneau and about forty of his Indian neighbors are successfully organizing a community credit union which will serve Indians and other interested parties throughout about 300 square miles of bush country. Local travel is still by canoe, bateau, small motor craft, or more frequently afoot. Though its shares are frequently bought and its loans repaid in furs or pelts, and though its headquarters change locations with the seasons, the Credit Union still thrives and serves, even in areas where the human census still averages about one per four square miles.

The Creek Farmers' Federal Credit Union of Bristow, Oklahoma, is a credit union of and for Negro farmers. Its members live within a fifteen-mile radius of Bristow, a town of about 6,000 in northeastern Oklahoma, about 30 miles from Tulsa.

Most of the members, currently about 400, are farmers, either full time or part time, though about 25 are professional people in other fields of earning. As in a great number of countrysides a majority of the residents supplement farming with other earnings. All live in the country and most grow subsistence crops, gardens, milk cows and pigs. Usually with the help of their families most of the Creek Farmers' members grow market crops —cattle, kaffircorn, sorghum molasses, in a few instances cotton. But the average member earnings from farms rarely exceed $1,500 per year; some are $750 or less. Several of the full time farmers earn $5,000 or more, but there are only about a dozen of the full timers who keep memberships in the credit union. About a fourth of the membership is of construction workers or other more or less regular wage earners who merely live in the country.

In other ways the pattern is contemporary America, where farming is getting to be more a part time than a full time occupation, where "job wages" are getting to be the number one cash crop, and where more and more town and city workers live in the country. But the Creek Farmers' Federal Credit Union shapes itself convincingly to the many ways and needs of the community. The credit union's work not only follows the farming seasons, it contributes to them and anticipates their needs. Oklahoma countrysides are wonderful to live in, but Oklahoma farming has its ups and downs. The downs are mostly droughts. The credit union can't keep them from happening but it does help the fields, gardens and pastures to become green and yield again. It helps the membership stay with a chosen way and place of life.

For every community mentioned here—white, as well as Negro or Indian—there are countless others where credit facilities are less than adequate. But Creek Farmers' Federal Credit Union illustrates again how an enlightened community can face up to its basic and prevailing need, and can fulfill a very substantial proportion of that need. In doing so, it signalizes a primary need, now become inter-American, and so far as the Free World is concerned, virtually global.

# *Credit Unions and the Eager Learners*

In the course of history one pre-eminent city usually demonstrates its prowess for influencing nations and raising or refusing to raise way-markers for what the more hopeful historians term "progress." Athens, Carthage and Rome were such epochal cities. So, in turn, were Paris and London and by more limited scope, Madrid, Tokyo, Bombay and Istanbul.

Now Washington, D.C., seems to be the premier international city of the present-day world. By no lucky accident or theorist's dream our own national capital and its 61.4 square miles of land, comprising the District of Columbia, has already acquired the greatest concentration of credit unions and several of the largest credit unions now in existence. It is true, of course, that Washington, D.C., has many other distinguishing characteristics. For one, it leads all American cities in numbers of churches and cathedrals. It has more public parks than any other city on earth. It is one of the memorable urban centers for racial integration. Currently it is the only major North American city where Negroes comprise an actual majority of the population.

For the political scientists the fast changing Potomac

town is a profound frontier of ideologies and changing social values. Any cogent onlooker should also note that along with other distinguishing traits Washington and the District lead all areas in percentages of credit union membership—already a third of the total census and rapidly going higher.

Federal employees as a group are the nation's and probably the world's nearest unanimous credit union members. More than half are now active members of credit unions, in most instances credit unions organized by and for workers in their own departments, bureaus, or services. Federal employees, as a great group, are no longer underpaid Americans. Their average incomes are increasingly above national averages. As giantism takes over our federal government, government workers are steadily gaining in salary status. Even Congressional salaries have been more than doubled in recent years and Congress now permits us to pay each member of Senate and House more than $40,000 per year for staff salaries. Quite probably, by totals, Washington now has the highest paid secretaries as well as the highest paid lawmakers in the world.

The ever growing roster of federal government employees with credit union memberships begins in the big white house at 1600 Pennsylvania Avenue which is also the rent-free home of the White House Employees Federal Credit Union with almost 600 members. The Treasury Department Federal Credit Union just across the wide street has more than twice that number. Treasury Department employees are world champion volume money handlers. At least 85 per cent of them are also shareholders in the U.S. Treasury credit union and more than half have borrowed from it rather recently.

More and more markedly the membership lists of Washington, D.C. credit unions approach identical status with the total employee lists. Our government sustains some of the nation's smallest credit unions and in terms of membership the nation's two largest. The Navy Federal with something like 27,000 members is now the world's biggest in membership. As this is written the area's second biggest is the Pentagon Federal with about 20,000 members and growing fast.

The list of important credit unions in Washington reads like a governmental structure chart. Among the distinguished middle-sizers is the State Department Federal, one of the strongest and best-seasoned of the old timers, with membership well above 90% of the current potential of 11,000 plus. There are credit unions, too, for employees in the Departments of Justice, Commerce, Agriculture, Interior, and Labor. There are good-sized credits unions in Civil Aeronautics, the Post Office Department, Public Health Service, the Bureau of Engraving and Printing, and the Library of Congress. Other typical medium-sizers are the National Archives, Bureau of Public Roads, Rural Electrification Administration, Federal Housing Authority, Bureau of the Census, and the oddly named Coast Guard Narcotics. Understandably but significantly the Internal Revenue is among the fastest growing. But the Senate and House of Representatives employees, who in terms of numbers are probably the world's highest paid government workers, have credit unions which are growing like Jack's beanstalk.

The District of Columbia has its own flowering of credit unions. Some of these, too, are big and strong, like the District Government Employees FCU, with upwards of 2,500 members, or the credit unions serving the Montgomery Teachers, the Uniformed Firemen, and the Capital Police. But hopefully and importantly our national capital also teems with small credit unions, many of outstanding promise. Examples include credit unions for the American Aviation Publications, the Capital Cab Drivers, and the Embassy Dairy. There are about 200 of these growing little ones. The St. Elizabeth Hospital Employees', with about 1,600 members, typifies the many institutional credit unions now in rational process of becoming middle-sized and useful. Howard University Employees Credit Union, as a facility of one of the great Negro universities, makes a special point of demonstrating good credit practices for the benefit of future Negro leaders.

Washington, D.C. is a backwash of many frontiers which gradually combine to create a sort of composite of their own peculiar brewing. The credit union has a far-reaching place in this improvised frontier. Washington is also a city of halves; half government employees and their immediate dependents and half employees of private industries, and as noted about half (52 per cent) Negro and almost half non-Negro. About half of all earners in the capital have incomes well above national averages and about half well below, though the average is now considerably above the national.

All these halvings bear importantly on credit unions. In earlier times and with fairly good reason most onlookers saw credit unions as a facility for the poor or financially under par; or as savings-lending facilities for communities beyond reach of banks. Washington now refutes these once reasonably accurate credos. Washington abounds with banks and commercial credit facilities, but by totals these cannot or do not fulfill the rapidly growing public needs for individual and community savings and credit.

The national capital has many poor people, as anyone can see from even a casual study of the retail merchandising establishment. The perennial epidemic of installment selling and the fantastic court loads of civil suits, petty claims, and garnishment writs, in all instances among the highest ever recorded, reiterate that the public needs for credit are intense and that prevailing concepts of credit use are very far from adequate. The lower wage earners need credit and far more credit unions than they now have. They need them as a source of money and an economic education.

By example, the Washington Telephone Employees Federal Credit Union is a once small-to-medium credit union which through helpful response to valid human needs has had bigness forced upon it. In early 1962 it listed over 6,000 members, over $2,000,000 in share and loan accounts. But while growing at a rate impressive even to capital dwellers, Washington Telephone has managed to remain human and personalized, primarily by virtue of its counseling service.

In the credit union's own handsome building, employees have the opportunity to talk privately with counselors in comfortable "visiting rooms." There they can trade their financial problems for expert advice. The novice dial girl who would invest in a wardrobe and a cosmetics cache designed to inspire Henry to propose, the temporary employee who seeks a means for financing maternity leave, the lineman who requires a quick loan for furnishing his new home, or the boys' club enthusiast who would provide the Battling Bobcats with a playing field and a part-time coach, all these and thousands more are subjects for counseling. The company co-operates with the credit union in making expert counselors available to all member employees; as a rule women advise women, men advise men.

Recently one of the most experienced counselors wrote: "In my eleven years of counseling I have noticed that credit union needs are above all else personal needs. Maybe that is why Washington is such a tremendous credit union town. It is otherwise perennially short of the personal touch. You find this cropping out in many ways. Our members are taking out more and more loans for buying books and art objects, for financing special studies and night courses, also for advancing church enterprises. There's a growing sense of community needs and values . . . and esteem for homes. Yesterday a dial girl received a loan of two hundred dollars to buy a Luciano water color. I personally know very little about water colors, but our girl knows a great deal. She wants the painting to help her establish a sense of feeling at home in her little apartment. So I recommended a *yes* to our credit committee. As I see it, the girl's contentment and feeling of being at home can be worth the two hundred dollars."

Telephone worker or federal worker, white or colored, the Washington employee visibly needs and benefits from his credit union. In prosperity as in poverty, part of the need is for a convenient facility for saving, borrowing and repaying. The need for consistent savings to supplement pensions or retirement income is also being felt increasingly. The community aspect of the credit union, even if minimized or stifled by excessive size, is another powerful factor of appeal and need. Finally there is the unending need for disinterested and unselfish advice about the problems related to money, the same need which has led credit unions collectively to launch through CUNA (Credit Union National Association) and member leagues a valiant program of family financial counseling.

Back of all these needs and beside them is the living demonstration of expert awareness on the parts of thousands of Washington public servants (principally those in the United States Treasury, Internal Revenue Department, federal lending and financing agencies and in other areas our career economists) that the credit union competently fulfills economic and advisory needs of a diverse but exceptional population.

Credit unions have always been engaged in family financial counseling. "The most important service of the credit union," Roy Bergengren once wrote, "is the education of the members in the management and control of their own money."

One man who knew Bergengren well, and who can also speak for the credit union movement of today and tomorrow, is Henry Claywell. Claywell is a plump, elderly man who manages Hillsboro County Teachers' Credit Union of Tampa, Florida's first teachers' credit union and one of the most successful in the South.

Henry Claywell would unquestionably be the last to term himself another Bergengren. "Sure, I seek the grail of economic democracy," he concedes, "But I'm no purple flash nor four-bit bargain. Back in Indiana I started out as a country boy who turned to country school teaching as a way of getting my own education. I came to Florida chasing after another schoolteacher I wanted to marry. So I married her and changed schools but I just keep on learning. . . ."

The learning stems largely from the $5,000,000 working capital and more basically from the 3,000 borrowers, and 6,500 active members of Hillsboro County Teachers' Credit Union. The other day an attractive young lady teacher strolled into the office to discuss her pending application for a loan to finance purchase of an original painting priced at $800. This, obviously, is a far cry from the loan objectives Henry Claywell grew up on—cash for painting the house, paying the dentist, burying Grandma Hannum, having a baby, or making a down payment on an auto which is both a conveyance and a symbol of earned equality and advancement.

The young teacher who would borrow to buy the original painting personifies still another changing goal of the credit union, which in Bergengren's words is to "prove in a modest measure the practicality of the brotherhood of man." But is the painting, which the young teacher would buy, really worth $800? In all honesty Henry (like the counselor in Washington) doesn't know. Neither, in all honesty, does any member of the credit committee on which he serves. But more relevantly none knows that the painting is *not* worth $800. Therefore, insofar as the young teacher qualifies as a shareholding, loan repaying member of the credit union, the answer already looks very much like a yes. Will the young teacher pay the loan of $800?

Henry Claywell and his fellow directors and committeemen have no doubt of it. "We believe the applicant has character. That's the extent of our real concern. Character is credit. Character is what ties yesterdays and tomorrows together. Something has to, you know."

Country schoolteachers Henry Claywell and his colleague, C. B. Morrill, felt that way back in August, 1933, when they each managed to raise $5 to become charter members and to finance the $2.50 fee for recording the charter of their proposed credit union, Florida's first for schoolteachers. After nine months they recruited seven other thin-pursed country schoolteachers who invested $5 each in shares, but during the next month 40 more joined. The assets which then totalled $300 were almost instantly subject to 54 loan applications; 37 of them presently to be granted. Passbook holder No. 1 and original Director Henry Claywell became treasurer-manager in 1937 and full time treasurer in 1941. But he never saw himself as a financier in any professional sense. His previous credit experience had consisted of borrowing and repaying an $80 loan and $50 interest on same.

As Henry Claywell sees them, credit unions and teaching are overlapping ways of life. He began to gain this perception in the early 1920's during his three years at the University of Indiana where he demonstrated talents for gentlemanly behavior, college journalism and falling in love. When his betrothed set out for Florida to teach school Henry followed her to Tampa where he passed the examination for a teacher's certificate and shortly took over a country school four miles from his beloved's and at the same $58 a month salary.

There were then 112 schools in the Hillsboro County Unit System and some 1,800 teachers whose positions in economic democracy were not elevated either by the teacher's salary laws or the depression which had struck Florida in 1926 instead of 1929. But as a teacher who married a teacher, Claywell nevertheless became a builder of economic democracy and a defender of the teaching profession, by means of one credit union, Hillsboro County Teachers'.

Like Bergengren, Henry Claywell is a family man who sees the family as the ultimate goal and inspiration of the credit union. Unlike Bergengren who evangelized a world cause by helping organize thousands of credit unions and serving all of them by devising laws and legislation for their authorization, Claywell is essentially a student and encourager of his own fellow members . . . "Man, you can't push people into credit unions or anything else. The most and best you can do is to encourage people to join in, on a personal and community basis. . . . As far as financial angles go, a loan can be an invaluable service or a ruinous disservice, depending on the competence or incompetence of the credit union itself."

Back in the early 1930's when Henry Claywell first

took to credit unioning, most Florida public schoolteachers were paid no more than $76 a month, and this frequently by voucher or warrant instead of actual spending money. Borrowing was inevitable. The loans were usually small in amount, in most instances anywhere from $10 to $200. But there was nothing small about the interest rates; and usury went with teaching like butter with hominy grits; $5 for the use of $50 for two weeks was typical. In those days and alas, even in these days, the only sure way a schoolteacher could get a bank loan was to prove beyond reasonable doubt that he or she didn't need the money!

For the teachers who did need the money the alternative was and is the loan shark. In Florida and elsewhere the earlier phrase for "loan shark" was the "salary buyer". In Florida of the 1930's, teacher loans were frequently made by process of salary buying. A victim would borrow his next month's pay in advance, and thereby permit the loan shark to move permanently into his line of earning. This abomination has now been made illegal in most states, including Florida. But no legislation pattern as yet has solved the fundamental problem of credit, which is rate of interest or "money wages" justifiable in a specific place or group. As sizes of loans increased (in Hillsboro Teachers, the now average loan is about $1,200, ten times the average of the middle 1930's), the establishment of just and reasonable interest rates becomes of itself a major crusade in economic and human justice.

About 500 of the 3,000 public schoolteachers in Hillsboro County, Florida, are Negroes. As a group the colored teachers require credit even more urgently than the white teachers. They must meet the rising educational standards of their profession and they must establish and maintain standards of self-respect, dress, social conduct, and community acceptance which are fully as high as those of the white teachers. It follows that prevailing credit needs of colored teachers exceed those of white teachers. Henry Claywell and his credit union colleagues respect the foregoing reality, and continue to serve all members in good faith and in turn.

The real story of Hillsboro County Teachers is far removed from the cliches of integration. It is rooted in the fundamental earth of democracy, of which credit unions are part; one can truly say in which they are implicit. Claywell, meanwhile, part teacher and counselor but mostly student, sits at his oversize cherrywood desk, eyes alert, lips shaping a half-smile as he states the case: "Man, credit union leadership is an art, not just for me and you, or the officers or hired help, it's an art for every man, woman and child in credit unions. That means millions, man; fact is, it means tens of millions; in time, hundreds of millions!"

Since the credit union is an institution of learning, it is less than astonishing that its associations with schools, are increasing, ranging from kindergartens to colleges, and that in the latter case such affinities are testified by credit unions at 150 different colleges and universities.

One of the more remarkable of these credit unions is connected with Suomi College of Hancock, Michigan. Suomi is a small "friendly sized" liberal arts junior college. It was founded in 1896 by the Finnish Evangelical Lutheran Church of America to meet the educational needs of Finnish people newly emigrated to the United States. The college began humbly in rented quarters in this Upper Peninsula countryside which was once the copper mining center of the world. The countryside is no longer a mining capital. Its great copper vents have found replacement on other continents. The Upper Peninsula is primarily a vacation land with winter sports facilitated by heavy snowfall and summertime charms enhanced by superb fishing, open forests and waters.

In 1900, while Finnish people worked the then Great Peninsula Copper Mines, the school raised its first building on a 150-foot lake front lot in Hancock town. At that time Suomi was a preparatory or "literacy" school for children of immigrant mine workers. As such the academy graduated its first class and added a Theological Seminary which presently became a training center for Lutheran ministers. During 1906 the modest but steadily growing academy established a commercial department which later grew into one of the area's most respected business schools. By 1923 the junior college was founded to meet rising educational needs of the region and people. The preparatory department was dropped and both the academy and seminary were presently taken over by the gallant little college.

Suomi College's credit union began along comparable lines of perceptive exploration. Actually it was not organized until late in 1958. During December of that year the proposed teacher-student credit union was approved and certified by the State of Michigan Banking

Department. The charter membership was opened wide to faculty, staff, directors, students and alumni of the college. Also to the immediate families of all the foregoing and to all accredited student organizations within the college. The entrance fee is the usual twenty-five cents, the minimum share holding is $5. Other customary precedents hold. The board of directors is regularly elected and includes representatives of all principal member groups. The three committees, credit, supervisory and educational are capable, well organized and operate along usual lines. The distinguishing feature is the open door policy and facilities which have placed the credit union in the heart structure of the college's life and works.

Suomi is a moderate-cost college. Financial aids are diverse, fairly numerous but quite modest. In the main the available scholarships range from $100 to $300 per year, the majority nearer $100. Student need for credit is quite real and continuous. The still fledgling credit union moves valiantly to meet these needs.

The task is far from easy. During its first 16 months, all of them hard going, the collegiate credit union made 31 loans totaling $6,605. Significantly 26 of these "pioneer" loans were to students, four to alumni and one to a college organization; none to faculty. During the tryout, shares totaled only $3,217. Accommodating the loans, which averaged about $120 apiece, required the judicious borrowing of $500 from a non-collegiate credit union.

The pattern of loan use is notable. Each of the four alumni received loans to complete his or her academic degree from a four-year college or university. The college organization which was granted a loan was the outdoors study group. All student loans helped keep worthy students in their academic programs at the junior college.

One instance was the story of Roy Tahtinen, who wished to buy a typewriter to better his college studies. The local typewriter dealer was not in position or mood to extend him credit. Roy applied for and received a loan of $140 from the Suomi College Credit Union. He bought the typewriter, used it effectively to improve his college work and raise his grade average to dean's list and scholarship eligibility level. For good measure the young man "took in" typing and used the earnings to repay the loan within nine months. Having completed his second year at Suomi, Roy applied for and received a second loan of $200 from the credit union to help finance his junior year at the four-year Pacific Lutheran College of Tacoma, Washington. This established a now maturing precedence for the changeover from student to alumni loans.

Up to the present time, the first goal of student loans has been to help students complete the basic junior college course. Jo Ann Pernu was a bright undergraduate with hopes of qualifying as a social worker. Jo Ann's father is an iron ore worker across in the big mines near Iron Mountain. When Jo Ann was within a semester of completing her basic college course, the mines were abruptly closed, as a result of a prolonged steel strike. Jo Ann's schooling and subsequent professional hopes seemed doomed. Her parents drove over to Hancock to take their daughter home with them.

More or less as an afterthought, the Pernus asked the Suomi Credit Union if there were any possibilities for granting the young lady a loan sufficient to finish her term. The credit union said yes, and after some figuring managed to advance the $400 required for completing her final semester. Within a week after graduation Jo Ann found a part-time job which enabled her to begin repaying the loan at the rate of $15 per month. When the steel strike ended her father was able to add to the payment. Following a summer of full-time work the loan was repaid in full. Jo Ann then returned to the college credit union, where she was able to borrow tuition money for an additional two years of study toward her degree in social work. Thus a career-blighting crisis in family earning was changed to a well-planned, solvent program of credit union borrowing and repaying. A Hancock banker notes, "Well, I darn sure admire the spunk of that little credit union and the good it does. . . . My bank couldn't have made any one of those loans. . . ."

One of the crucial problems after getting through college is the crossing over from classroom and lecture hall to the routine ways of workaday earning and living. At last and at best, commencement means beginning. As more and more millions of college graduates keep finding out, "commencement" raises problems additional to those of adjusting the length of the graduation gown or keeping the cap tassel on the appropriate side of the head.

The weeks or months immediately following graduation often find the erstwhile collegian at a financial crisis.

The financial strain of getting through college has been long and debilitating to the Old Man. However generous of impulse the parental coffers are almost inevitably low. Through the theoretically carefree college years Pop has given and advanced, borrowed and otherwise parted with earnings and savings. As a rule younger brothers and sisters are waiting their turns for the adventure in ivied walls. Yet the transition from college to employment or professional establishment almost invariably requires still more spending.

Marlene Barri, who recently completed the Suomi College course in secretarial studies, found herself a secretarial job in the Big City, in this instance, Milwaukee. Marlene was resolved to take her widowed mother with her. This required money for necessary clothing, train fare and meals, hotel accommodations and down payment on an apartment. All were required and, alas, due before issue of the first pay check. Like hundreds of thousands of eager young graduates, Marlene lacked conventional credit sources or approachable note signers. She had no banking connections or pre-established credit base. She turned to the Suomi College Credit Union for a loan of $175; the sum was readily and graciously advanced, and in the same manner it is being repaid.

On its official letterheads, Suomi College, with a current enrollment of about 175 students, quotes the editors of *Who's Who in America:* "Small schools in relation to their enrollment have contributed the highest percentage of graduates to the pages of *Who's Who in America.*" The Suomi College Credit Union confidently sets out to prove that the small college with students of extremely modest means or none at all can also build excelling solvency rates and usefulness quotients in the cooperative lending function of the credit union.

The challenge is formidable. Many or most borrowers are minors. The majority lack, and are months or years away from, regular employment. Moral responsibility must transcend legal responsibility. But the still swaddling, loan-ladened and cash-short Suomi College Credit Union is winning. As yet it is unable to pay salaries or wages to any of its principals. All guidance work, accounting, auditing and customer services remain gratis. Yet, remarkably enough, it paid a token dividend even during its infant year when loan applications exceeded shares at least ten to one.

Not one of the loans has conventional security. Even by the most liberal interpretation no more than a third of the loans could possibly comply with even minimum banking "standards". Because student needs are still far more urgent than faculty needs, the great majority of loans are going to students and alumni, preponderantly to new graduates.

Meanwhile, the student-faculty-alumni-staff credit union has time and work on its side, also youth, courage and a tradition of use of muscle, mind and spirit. Other good harvests are materializing. The one-for-all, all-for-one credit union is combining the goals of helping students during their academic time at Suomi College, with helping them become established in advance study or career work; this plus the usual help and advantages for faculty and staff members, extending to the always important ties with alumni.

A story from Arkansas also demonstrates that big blessings can come in small packages. These particular blessings are dispensed by the Employees' Credit Union of the Central Transformer Company of Pine Bluff, Arkansas. Plant Manager G. A. Smith explains how things used to be: "We pay workers on Friday afternoons. Beginning shortly after lunch time the sheriff or one of his deputies used to sit outside the paymaster's office to serve wage attachments—up to twenty attachments every Friday. Arkansas law allows wage attachments up to 89 per cent of total earnings. Personally I never could figure out how any worker could live on the 11 per cent of earnings which the garnishee law leaves him. But a lot of our very good employees have done just that. . . ."

They did, that is, until 1956 when the Central Transformer's Employees' Credit Union began swinging into action. Within the year the garnishments dropped to about one-tenth the previous average; the present score is a heartening zero. As 1955 ended the credit union's total income from interest was only $1.22; the net operating loss was $8.78. However, one month later the share holdings climbed to $2,000 and loans outstanding $1,043. By the end of 1956 the membership stood at 173, out of a total employee personnel of 290. The sheriff no longer camps at the paymaster's door come Friday afternoon. This flourishing credit union, too, is in its own way an institution of learning.

In broader reckoning, all the world is a school for credit unions and those who would found or serve and benefit from them.

[ 8

# *Credit Unions and the New Frontiers*

In these times when accredited facts change, disappear or reappear as readily and rapidly as official boundaries or governments of actions, the word "frontier" receives a great deal of hard use and pushing around. By routine dictionary definition "frontier" means primarily, the border of a national territory; secondarily, "the farthest civilized output beyond which lie unsettled or savage regions."

The United States provides a now classic demonstration of the fact that literal frontiers cannot endure as such. Granted that it was born more of a vast and attainable abundance of free or inexpensive lands than of any theorist's dream, American democracy can no longer endure and mature in that manner. We no longer have tax-free or inexpensive lands to turn to for escape from the forces which could destroy our freedom.

Our literal or as some say horizontal frontiers moved westward until they tumbled into the Pacific. But there are now other frontiers, almost infinitely magnified: frontiers of near and outer space, frontiers of needed production, frontiers of justice, enlightened economics, and human dignity. These frontiers are attainable by means already at hand and in great part proved.

If other economic institutions have lost the sight and spirit of the builder of frontiers, as some say they have, then it is doubly fortunate that credit unions have not. Our free enterprise system now struggles against formidable odds.

The great American frontier of the 1860's was vehemently wealth-seeking. Its credit structure was exotic and in no little part piratical. At best, the concept of credit during the 1860's was not cooperative. Paper loaded and virtually without legal controls, frontier banking was a procedure of giving the least and grabbing the most. Usury was not only permissible; it was orthodox. Ten per cent per month was a not unusual interest rate during the 1860's; 25 per cent per year was a howling bargain. Buffalo Bill Cody recorded that in 1862 he was obliged to borrow $40, that he paid $20 per month interest for five months and ended up by still owing the $40, which he finally repaid with a "fine Shawnee saddle horse."

Times have changed, but certainly not enough, on the frontier of economic democracy. Not long ago in Orange County, South Carolina, a 33-year-old Negro secretary had paid a small loan company a total of $813 in interest and principal on a $75 maternity loan made to the secretary's mother back when the secretary was being born. Prior to her daughter's coming of age, the mother had paid interest totalling $411 on the same $75 loan. After the daughter became office manager of a Charleston law firm she found counsel and courage to tell the lender where he could go. The story would be much happier if more such endings could be reported. Or if the tragedy of loan sharking were less omnipresent.

The loan shark is not restricted to any state or region, but as a matter of known records his predatory forays are frequently directed toward the Negro, Indian, Spanish American or the very poor white, or combinations of all four. The Negro suffers most. In seven southern states where Negroes represent 21.8 per cent of the current census, somewhat less than two-tenths of one per cent of outstanding bank loans are being made to Negroes. The immediate effects of course, is to throw the colored applicants to the loan sharks. Yet to qualify for and justify their places in a democracy our colored citizens as a group actually need credit more urgently than our white citizenry.

The paradox is continued in various credit agencies of our Federal government, including the Federal Housing Authority and the Home Owners Loan Corporation. The actual intentions of these and other Federal lending agencies are rarely discriminatory, but discrimination rises from their basic ground rules. Actual percentages of home ownership by Negroes, Indians and certain other racial minorities are increasing, though the average values and upkeep of their residential properties are still below par. But in terms of adequate improvements, inferior locations remain a serious barrier to sufficient and otherwise justifiable mortgage credit.

On the commercial side, so-called small business loans made by the Federal Government have very largely bypassed Indians, Negroes, and all other racial minorities in the United States. Actually the so-called small business loans are misnamed, some say, since "small business" is described as enterprises with capital structures ranging from $50,000 upward. This, of course, is far above and beyond collateral facilities of most businesses owned by Negroes, Indians, or Spanish Americans, or, indeed, by most of the rest of us.

In Durham, North Carolina, a Negro war veteran and law school graduate named Floyd McKissick set out to learn not only the salient facts of credit abuses and evasions suffered by his people, but to find some attainable remedies. He soon observed that along with the usual American needs for adequate standards of food, clothing, and shelter, Negroes needed an opportunity to establish and build up useful businesses qualified for serving Negroes and white people alike. He noted that again and again the more talented members of the Negro communities were leaving for other fields of employment. One after another as his sisters married, they left with their husbands who were able to command better professional positions in the North and East.

But on the home scene he noted that the primary causes of failure of businesses owned by Negroes seemed to be chronic shortage of available credit. One instance was the promising beginning of a small chemical factory which sought to specialize in the manufacture and distribution of sprays, disinfectants, herbicides and similar products needed by local farmers and dairymen. The chemical plant was well planned and competently built. Both its proprietors were intelligent and industrious young men, well schooled in chemistry. Their immediate cause of failure was in the area of advertising and selling. Substantial outgoes of money were required. When the first severe credit pinch developed, the credit was not available. Advertising and supporting sales efforts faltered as a result. The business went bankrupt. Both proprietors were obliged to leave home and find jobs in a larger chemical plant, which cannot fill the special local needs for which the smaller venture was specifically designed.

Floyd McKissick regretted the enforced exodus of these two proprietors, useful men whom the community could not afford to lose. A no less regrettable failure dealt with the passing of a Negro-owned country store which had specialized in supplying the special needs of tobacco farmers of the area. An over-optimistic expansion of stock coupled with a severe slump of farm prices for tobacco and hogs combined to snap the existent credit lines. None of the local banks saw fit to advance the needed credit. The storekeeper was obliged to file a petition for bankruptcy. All suffered as a direct result.

Citing such instances, McKissick insists that the most decisive need of the Negro today is the legitmate opportunity to establish and manage enterprises which serve public needs, to serve any or all publics, and thereby to win friends, to qualify for leadership and develop a more adequate calibre of Negro leaders.

Late in 1959 McKissick was elected president of the local Business and Professional Chain, one of the older chapters of a national association for Negro business and professional men. The great educator and leader, Booker T. Washington, founded it back in 1911. The name of the national organization has recently been changed to the National Business League. But the goal supports Booker T. Washington's thesis that the Negro deserves, requires or seeks no advantage or disadvantage based on race; that he requires only a fair and rational chance to prove himself on a basis of competence in his work and as a patriot.

In an effort to project a remedy for the credit shortage, McKissick and some 200 fellow members of the Durham Chain began a concerted search for and study of needed enterprises which their members are qualified to provide. One of the self-apparent needs was revival of the chemical firm. Another was a new countryside store for the tobacco farmers. Another was a "Wash-o-Mat" where women could bring their home laundry. There was a long-standing need, too, for a good drive-in restaurant.

McKissick and his fellow officers agreed that these needs deserved top billing. But as usual, credit was essential. So a special meeting was called to discuss the possibilities and advantages of a credit union to be founded, built and used by Chain members.

Members voted to try it and to enter formal application for a state charter. The Chain Credit Union began work early in May, 1960, with an initial membership of 39 and share issues totalling about $700. Within a month the membership dues and shareholdings were large enough to accommodate a first handful of loans to members. These were modest loans; the largest was $400, but all were thoughtfully directed toward fulfillment of the goal of helping Negroes to serve the public.

From the beginning the Chain's credit union has supplemented the usual unpaid officers and committeemen of the credit union with a special committee of the whole to seek out local business openings or possibilities. The committee makes analyses of possible markets, products to be developed, and managerial needs and tax problems.

It is common agreement that shareholdings must total at least $300,000 before the credit union can accommodate some of the credit needs already visualized. As this is written, the share total is growing steadily but is still short of this amount. Meanwhile, the initial list of approved loans is in keeping with the planning. The credit union has not been able as yet to undertake total financing of any enterprise. But it has ably supplemented and safeguarded enterprises by providing a credit source for "second phase" needs, which in many instances decide the failure or success of small businesses. In its first year no loan ended in default and no enterprise failed. Floyd McKissick and his fellow credit builders grant that in the very nature of small business enterprises, risks are real and formidable. In keeping with well-known averages, some ventures will fail. Most probably, some loans will be lost, or repayments deferred. But all are satisfied that the credit union has proved a valid enterprise.

McKissick states matter of factly, "I see the credit union as a group facility for helping its members help themselves. I have never believed that democracy is any theorist's dream. Like man himself, democracy, as I see it, is a creation with immortal spirit and mortal body. The last named is bound to be economic as well as social. In any free enterprise system, credit must feed the living body of democracy. The credit union is one of the better ways to produce credit and appease the natural hunger. But I begin to notice that the credit union, in actual operation, goes beyond the fulfillment of this absolute need. It helps bring together people as a community working together. The basis here is not of race, creed or color but rather the special needs of the group from any cause. The community of interest which any credit union represents is in very real part social and spiritual. So is the creation and good use of credit. . . ."

A similar conviction was recently stated by the pastor of a small-town Methodist church in Northern Ohio. Not long ago the men's club of the congregation presented to the pastor and his board of elders a recommendation that a credit union be organized within the congregation.

Their specific needs are varied, but on the whole typical. The town recently lost one of its principal industries. Local unemployment, though relieved by the recent coming of a new industry, remains quite real and for some of the congregation distinctly painful. About a third of the congregation are elderly people living on Social Security allotments or other pensions.

A major credit need was presented by the church renovation program, which began more than a year before the credit union. Approximately 20 of the members required loans for fulfillment of pledges already made. At least as many more had expressed their willingness to increase their contribution if a credit facility could be made available. But a conservative minority still held that the function of a church is to receive offerings, not to participate in producing or providing them.

The pastor's first move was to request the president of the men's club to make a detailed study of the needs of a church credit union and the exact procedures for organizing it. Then a regular midweek evening service was converted to an open forum for discussion and appraisal of needs, ways and means. At the meeting approximately 200 members, or somewhat more than one-fourth of the congregation, expressed interest not only in having a credit union but in actively joining it. Only seven opposed.

A slate of temporary officers was placed in nomination from the floor and the pastor found himself unanimously elected an acting director, and with a local public accountant as acting treasurer. Two local businessmen and the pastor's wife were elected as a temporary organization committee.

Within one week after the charter had been granted, membership stood at 226 and shareholdings totalled $7,245. During the second week following member election of regular officers and key committeemen, a first "honor roll" of fourteen loans was granted, for an average of $53 each. The honor roll was well named; every one of the charter loans has been repaid punctually.

The church credit union is now open for business three afternoons weekly in an improvised office in the church basement. As yet no voice of opposition has been heard and Ohio's Protestant Credit Union No. 24 is clearly succeeding. Now that it has grown to a size and stature sufficient to justify printed stationery, the supervisory committee is in the market for a suitable motto. The best suggestion to date is "Democracy in Credit: God directing, People Benefiting."

In Ohio as elsewhere, the church credit union faces an increasingly emphatic challenge as the temporal as well as spiritual obligations of all churches continue to increase and expand. In Ohio as in practically all states, one meets sincere if conservative church members who still believe that a church credit union, even though not housed within the church building and not active on the Sabbath tends to desecrate the House of God with the fact or intent of "money changing." This view, of course, is legitimately rooted in Christian history and is still subject to honest differences of opinion. But in any event, God's churches must still stand for and dutifully heed the needs of man as well as the will of God. In more and more instances the credit union is being accepted and accredited as a facility of fulfillment.

For example, in another section of Ohio not long ago, a church-member credit committee considered a loan application which gave as "Purpose of Loan" this bizarre answer: "Changing big rocks to little rocks." After recovering from the initial astonishment they unhesitatingly granted a $450 loan to develop and build a ball-and-ring mill for pulverizing waste stone.

The applicant was a young-hearted old-timer enduring forced retirement at 69, who prefers for reasons of his own at this writing to be called Mr. X. During his quarter century as a quarry worker, Mr. X was appalled by the formidable wastes which are common to that industry. In commercial quarrying of building stone, 60 per cent is the usual waste or discard ratio. For granite, 80 to 85 per cent is average; for building marble, around 70 per cent. Within a few years a sizable commercial quarry either produces one or more unwanted mountains of "grout" or waste rock, or spends veritable fortunes hauling it away.

For several years before retirement, Mr. X directed a series of enterprises for utilizing waste quarry rock. These included conveyor-fed hammer mills which break up the grout into gravels or chips for such uses as pavement mixes and surface sprinkling for asphaltic shingles. These hammer mills also enabled the quarry to produce fine rock chips for use in filtering municipal water supplies, and to convert the colored or tinted marble to fragments for use in Terrazo-style permanent flooring. These milling devices Mr. X conceived or invented, without benefit of special training or degrees in mechanical engineering.

Following retirement Mr. X spent considerable time at developing a ball-and-ring mill which would further pulverize gravel and change it to rock flour. The principle is that of crushing little rocks into infinitesimal rocks by means of a powered gyrator which forces the gravel into lines or circles of ball bearings confined in strong steel rings. The rock flour is readily salable for a growing variety of uses, including the manufacture of pottery wares, molding clays, stone putties, roof menders, sizing or fillers for rubber goods, and so on. In general, the finer the stone is pulverized the more valuable it becomes.

Mr. X knows a great deal about credit unions, as well as rocks. At one time or another he has been a member of five credit unions, a director of two, president of one, and a credit committee member for three. He is sometimes acting treasurer for his current church credit union and for this service he is paid exactly what the regular treasurer is paid, which is "no money, much pleasure, many friends." For almost 30 years Mr. X has been buying credit union shares, re-investing dividends in shares, borrowing and repaying loans. In bygone years he has received loans for furnishing and refurnishing homes, buying autos, sending and helping send his own and other children to college, building and stocking pigeon roosts, rehabilitating a prison parolee, and many other individual but worthwhile enterprises.

"I like the idea of making something worthwhile which wasn't worthwhile before," says Mr. X, holding up a glass vial filled with marble which his own mill and enterprise have reduced to what the trade calls "sugar-size diameters," this for use in the manufacture of a paint-or-ink removing soap. "Also I like credit unions," Mr. X concluded. "I have one to thank for this little jag of a rock mill business . . . and a lot besides. Back when I was a mere boy, not hardly 35 years old, a credit union helped me settle down to a worthwhile family life. All during my middle age stretch other credit unions gave me all kinds of interests, including a lot of helped and helpful friends . . . Now that I'm supposed to be old, a credit union helps me grow young again."

Mr. X reached for his Ohio-style cob pipe. "Credit unions are good for all ages. But probably best for us that the calendar records by mistake as being old . . . Way I see it, that's all part of the talent of credit unions for bringing out values which otherwise wouldn't or couldn't be."

"In Indiana" says an old-time Hoosier treasurer, "the

credit unions get a specially big volume of what I call 'hanker' business. Members hanker for this and that; old glass collections, home laboratories and workshops, book collections, antiques—particularly furniture. Indiana is still a cabinetmaker's and furniture collector's heaven. We do a remarkable amount of business with home or hobby manufactures of just about everything, from fly swatters to fraternity jewelry. But this hankering to own, restore and cherish old and true things of Indiana is getting to be a banner background for our most successful loans."

Jim Nutley, an Indianapolis high school teacher, takes the same view. In his earlier years of teaching Jim was a vocational education instructor and supervisor of "shop" at Whittier high. When he married and transferred to Central, there happened to be an urgent need for a physics instructor. At his wife's urging and the principal's, Jim filled the vacancy. Though he had shone in both the physics courses he had taken at Indiana University, Jim dipped into savings to take a summer refresher course. When he had finished it, there were no more savings to dip into.

The following vacation found the bride and groom with a mutual urge to trail down a summer's job. Jim chose instead to spend the summer at self-directed shop work. By gradual stages he and his bride, whose hobby is antique furniture, attended enough country auctions to acquire a nucleus of old-time furniture for the most part authentic but, as the saying goes, "beat up."

Jim borrowed $200 from his teachers' credit union. He spent about $50 for varnish, paints, brushes and a few hand tools, used the rest for living expenses while he and his wife put in an effective summer restoring furniture for the house they began buying the following fall. Having repaid the loan from salary checks, Jim borowed $500 for use the following summer vacation. With this he completed a reasonably effective home workshop and fell to restoring two more carefully purchased suites of auctioned furniture.

With their new home attractively furnished and mostly by way of their home workshop, the Nutleys are using their teachers' credit union to finance regular summer employment as collectors and restorers of antique furniture. In the past three years the couple have become professionals in both respects—as teachers and as self-propelling finders and restorers of old furniture.

In old Quebec, Louis Chalfont still keeps what he fondly terms his Old Paris Food Market, as his father did before him. The continuation of his market depends on a local and sturdy credit union which lends to Louis and several of his competitors. Similarly, in Montreal, no less than 100 old-style French-Canadian food markets are surviving and thriving despite modernity and the chain store invasion.

Down in North Miami, Florida, the Peoples Credit Union established by "Pop" Rentfro has helped members establish many home enterprises, from commercial rose gardens and orchid "dens" to sea shell shops and road stands. A young Indian borrowed to stake his reservation kin to a "start" of good cattle. A local enthusiast for bayou fishing joined a Seminole friend, and borrowed from the Peoples Credit Union to finance the building of half a dozen "air-boats," small flat-bottomed boats propelled by deck-mounted auto engines which turn airplane propellers. Conventional motorboats are worse than useless in the bayous and root-snarled waters of the near-by Everglades. But the Everglades are largely open to air-boat travel. Magnificent fishing and nature study make air-boat tours a valid and profitable catering.

A continent's width away from the space frontiers of Florida, one encounters a different kind of frontier in California, where the residents are increasing too rapidly for the instant capacity of any tabulating machine. Every month 30,000 additional families are said to settle in California.

Back of the spectacular and sometimes terrifying new growth of California, one senses awareness of its great antiquity. This is symbolized by California's famed bristlecone pine, one of the oldest living things on earth; its age is believed to be at least 4,500 years. The sequoia or redwood trees, according to some scholars, were living at least 15 centuries before the birth of Christ.

The Great Valley, one-time desert between the Sierra Nevadas and the Coastal Range, now cradles an amazing new era of super-harvests raised from longer-living roots. Indeed many experts see here a development of root longevity and hardiness which will eventually change a great many of our annual crops to perennials.

Back of and under this new concept of root power is a veritable magicians' field day of farming advances, many of which are being expedited by credit unions. New chemical compounds are being used to delay or hasten harvests according to market needs; to enable orchard trees to set heavy, light or medium harvests as desired, or to shed excessive fruit loads on their own power. Chemists are perfecting non-contaminating soil fumigants which repress or destroy most root enemies. Also developed and in widespread use are plant metabolism upsetters, which destroy weeds by causing them to grow themselves to death. Engineers have developed machines which compress nitrogen in the air and ready it for feeding directly to crop roots via irrigation water.

California's imaginative green-thumbers now visualize a bonanza of staple vegetables, including green peas, snap beans, cucumbers, squashes and other commercial vegetables, fortified with food-storing perennial roots comparable to those of asparagus. Particularly in California's Great Valley, vegetable farmers envisage hardy melon vineyards bearing bumper harvests of fancy melons year after year, also vineyards or orchards of perennial tomatoes, pod peas, green beans and many other long-lived bearers. All this is more than pipe-dreaming. It is based on the now firmly accredited scientific convictions (a) that healthy vegetative roots are or can be made virtually immortal and (b) that relatively healthy vegetative roots are definitely attainable.

All this is typical frontier talk. But it carries the ring of accomplishment. Though a third of it is desert and another third is rugged mountain, California is already and by far our greatest farming state. It easily leads the nation in total yields and values of orchard and other perennial crops. It ranks high in such staples as cattle, cotton, potatoes, cereal grains and green vegetables. In terms of total value of harvests it is regularly hundreds of millions of dollars ahead of Iowa, the next contender among farming states.

Appropriately, California also leads in numbers, assets, and loan activities of credit unions. Even while nine-tenths of these California credit unions take their subsistence from established pay rolls, others are participating directly in the imaginative business of working the land. At root level the largest and most productive of American frontiers is a frontier of credit—enterprising, inventive, and personalized.

At Modesto a credit union treasurer told about one cherished member whose business is that of a "reawakening" wastelands. This useful citizen drives his Jeep into the rough dry land at the bases of nearby mountains and locates strips of earth which no ordinary man would look at more than once. Jim Tolly looks at them many times and borrows from his credit union to buy strips of terrestial junk yards which he "somehow likes the looks of."

His first move is to hire a bulldozer tractor to scoop away the more movable surface boulders. He then destroys the ranker desert bush with chemical herbicides and plants the hard, gypsum-infested earth with hardy desert grasses or "three-awns" which gradually add humus to the soil and serve to establish soil texture. After five years or so he scrapes over the plantings with a tractor-drawn disc harrow, then uses a special blower-drill to plant the wastelands with seed of rugged, perennial range grasses. After these growths have further added to the soil's nutrition and further lowered its load of gypsum and other toxic elements and built up its fertility still more, he "rough plows" and fertilizes the land, then plants hardy range grasses such as grama or buffalo or bluestem. Within another ten years the once useless land is capable of growing premium range grasses, even alfalfa. Thus one-time "junk land" gains fifty fold, even a hundred fold in value. Tolly finances with successive credit union loans averaging about $900 apiece, repays promptly, covers each successive borrowing with another purchase of shares.

Down in the irrigated orchard lands near Modesto lives Alton Drake, an ardent credit union participant who invents and builds heat chambers for immunizing young fruit trees from bud and root viruses. By heating the newly dug nursery stock to controlled temperatures high enough to destroy the enemy virus without injuring the tissues of the young trees, Drake's orchardist customers find it possible to reduce the usual seven-year "wait over" ordinarily required for bringing newly planted fruit trees to bearing age to three years, or at most four.

At Lonar a credit union treasurer remembers a loan application from an aircraft worker who recently borrowed $700 for starting a weed farm. This consists of a five-acre plot which the member purposely crowds with about 100 varieties of principal weed pests. He sells the weed seeds, or in some instances the roots, to manufacturers of chemical weed killers and herbicides; he also sells "on-the-scene killing rights."

The Great Valley's "revolution of abundance" is attracting agronomists and other expert appraisers from all over the world. These and other students quickly note that practically all independent farmers in the Great Valley face a common requirement; they must keep increasing and improving harvests in order to stay in business. For example, Fresno County, about 185 miles below San Francisco, now leads the U.S. and the world in total value of its farm crops. Many of its 5,985 square miles which first settlers tried sometimes vainly to sell at 25 cents an acre now produce crops worth $5,000 or more per acre each year. Irrigation, better mechanization and plant breeding, effective transcontinental marketing, superior management have multiplied land values.

Sam Edwards, a director of the San Joaquin Packers' Credit Union has succeeded with two allegedly impossible crops, figs and almonds. Like many of his farmer neighbors Edwards drives a Cadillac, employs a foreman with a Ph.D., and a five-digit salary. He equips his farm hands with Geiger counters to keep track of radioactive tracers regularly used to check up on the effectiveness of fertilizers and sprays, and gives the hired help frequent leaves to brush up on subjects such as sub-cellular biology, virology and cell anatomy. Edwards reflects, "When I went to agricultural school thirty years ago the professors told us there's no such thing as healthy vegetation. They believed and taught that the vegetable kingdom, though it sustains the animal, is just naturally the sickly kingdom. . . . We can't go along with that, nowadays. We have to grow healthy crops or get out of business. Healthy crops cost a lot of money and require a lot of credit. The way I see it the credit union is more important to a farmer than his seed store. . . ."

Tom Adams, down San Diego way, is an incorrigible frontiersman who faces up to this inevitability of today's and tomorrow's frontier. Tom was born and raised on a forty-acre fruit farm which now includes three suburban developments now fully developed, seven big service stations, two supermarkets, a laundromat center and so on. Tom Adams remains a farmer at heart and in fact, but it isn't easy. When his father died back in the early 1930's, Tom set out to settle the little estate, of which he was administrator, fairly and squarely to all concerned. Then entered the lawyers and the distant but acquisitive relatives. Tom retreated to the 12 acres he had managed to save and went back to market gardening. But taxes and tolls of "improvement districts" grew more rapidly than Tom's vegetables or fruit crops.

When the petroleum company knifed into his most promising apricot grove and his best root vegetable lands to make way for still another super-duper filling station, Tom took part of the money the tax collectors overlooked and invested it in credit union shares. When the supermarket people began pressuring him to sell four acres for a market center site with parking facilities on the side, Tom sold them all that remained of his ancestral acres except the location site for a roadside vegetable stand. He invested 20 per cent of the money in credit union shares and used the rest to buy a 20-acre hillside "ranch" which previously had never grown anything except tumbleweed, scratch grass and controversy.

With the help of his credit union Tom Adams is now changing the erstwhile desert fringe into a highly productive vegetable farm. His first borrowing of $2,000 went to drilling an irrigation well; he hit a good one at 203 feet. His next $1,000 loan, also secured by shareholdings, went for routine soil improvement including successful plantings of alfalfa and other clovers. A first three acres duly irrigated and planted to root vegetables and "greens" paid interest charges and financed a temporary home which Tom is gradually expanding with his own labor. He now has nine acres in bearing, three wells, one full time hired man and a successful roadside market–located on his former, gulped-up homestead.

As a credit union member and director Tom Adams admits a strong preference for "borrowing and repaying my own money instead of pussyfooting with bankers and mortgages." In another two years and with another two "waterin' wells" he expects to have approximately 18 of his 20 acres in profitable bearing. This is a reasonable and promising likelihood, not an absolute certainty. But Tom Adams admits one absolute certainty. He is using a good credit union and his own good and experienced work to cause value to exist where it never existed before and otherwise might never be. Tom suggests that quite probably in final analysis this is the true goal of all credit unions and, indeed, of all frontiers.

# *Credit Unions and the Hungry People*

If anyone should doubt that credit unions are made of different stuff than other financial institutions, let him look south into Latin America. A powerful story is unfolding there.

South America may well be the greatest unopened treasure chest remaining on earth. It has the longest and highest mountain chain in the world. Its foothills and deserts conceal vast and undeveloped mineral resources. Behind the mountains, enormous traces of workable land stand idle for lack of transportation. Unexplored and unmeasured tropical forests hold the promises of virtually limitless wealth. And besides all these, there is the greatest water supply in the world. Ocean liners can steam 2,500 miles up the Amazon, which pours three times as much water into the sea as the Mississippi. The Rio de la Plata, too, has twice the Mississippi's volume. There is unused water power enough to spin the earth.

Populations have always been sparse, compared with more crowded continents. By contrast, nearby nations include several of the most densely populated land surfaces on the globe. Haiti and El Salvador are said to rank among world leaders in terms of numbers of people per habitable square mile of land. But South America in terms of resources has long challenged Africa as the most underpopulated of continents.

Now populations are catapulting. In terms of proportionate census increase, South America probably leads all the continents during the early 1960's. Census experts are convinced that South America "has room for"—and resources potentially adequate to support—at least half a billion people. But already United Nations authorities, along with officials of such governments as Brazil and Argentina, are predicting that if current population growth continues in keeping with expert forecasts, South America will have its 500 million people by the end of the present century.

According to the best current estimates the total South American "product"—industrial, agricultural, mineral, and consumer goods outputs—is increasing at an average rate of about 4.5 per cent annually. This is far behind the census increase, hardly within seeing distance of vivid human needs already recognized. The inadequacy is accentuated by the fact that in average ages Latin Americans now comprise many of the youngest publics in the present-day world. Today and from all rational appearances for years to come, the average citizen age in Latin America is well under 30 years. In Venezuela, Brazil and Ecuador it is currently estimated as between 26 and 29 years. The meaning in terms of absolute human need is self evident. The crucial need is for the means with which to grow.

These needs are essentially economic, and are not essentially social. As the schoolbooks unfailingly tell us, the South American republics had a common colonial history, a common movement for independence, and then a common form of government. Ecuador, Peru, and Bolivia are typical of the *del sur* countries which emerged with predominantly Indian populations. Argentina and Uruguay, and Costa Rica, are predominantly white. In Brazil there is a generous admixture of Negro blood. When the new republics were formed by the liberators, slaves were freed and the Indians received the same political rights as the whites. But not economic rights. While never segregated socially, the Indian has always been exploited by the whites economically.

All over South America you find the same system of great landed estates. Most of the good land, from the mountains to the sea, delivers its produce to support an absentee landlord who lives in luxury in the city. You may travel for days to cross one such hacienda. In such a society, our needy worker can find employment on the land only as a day laborer, or as a renter who can be uprooted summarily, or as one who scratches a living from rocky and unwanted soil higher up in the mountains—land to which there may be no way to acquire a title.

When such a man needs money to repair his roof or to buy a plow, where can he get the money? Certainly not from the established banking facilities. Even if a Peruvian Indian should somehow find his way to the city and should enter a bank seeking to borrow 500 sols (about $20), the bank is forbidden by law to grant his loan. If anybody lends him the money, it will be the usurer, the money lender who may charge rates of 20 per cent or even 50 per cent per month. The need must indeed be desperate for a borrower to take such a risk. On a loan of this size he may spend a lifetime in debt, still owing the full amount after paying back many times the borrowed sum.

If anything, Father Dan McLellan, M.M., found the situation worse than described in 1950 when he came to Puno, 12,000 feet high in the Andes of Peru. Here he came to minister to a community of Quechua and Aymara Indians, descendants of the storied Incas, whose empire had stretched from Ecuador to Chile and Argentina long before the bearded Spaniards sailed to the New World. Their ancestors had ruled the continent from their mountain top citadels, but now Father Dan found these proud people living in floorless mud huts, diseased and hungry. They lived by raising potatoes and a few scrawny animals. Seldom did their income exceed $100 per year. Silent and suspicious, they had rejected every gesture of aid from outside with open scorn.

Father Dan was not one to give up easily. He had been a popular student in high school, a star football player, and finally an amateur boxer of such talent that he once considered turning professional. By the time he finished seminary training to become a Maryknoll Father, he had also learned to fly. It took a man who would try anything to win over Puno.

While the Indians looked on from a distance, Father Dan started his labors. He began to hold services in the ancient but almost abandoned church for the few curious enough to attend. He learned his first words in the Quechua language. He established a domestic arts course for wives, a demonstration plot for farmers, and a recreational program for the youth. He gave medicine to the sick. He became an amateur magician to win the friendship of the children, and through them the good will of their parents. When none of these produced results rapidly enough to suit him, he tried a grandstand play. Realizing that even the most sullen and impassive Indian had the same passionate love for bullfighting as all the rest, Father Dan stepped into a bullring and risked his life to win the cheers of the crowd by his bravery before the snorting charges of the bull. That did it. To Father Dan's delight, his church was full every Sunday thereafter. It had taken nearly five years.

Meanwhile, the persistent padre had learned enough about his Indians and their needs to get 23 of them to start a credit union. After a series of meetings to explain its purpose and self-help character, the San Juan Parish Credit Union started with an original capital of 600 sols (less than $30). The first loan was 300 sols for a sewing machine, made to a man who was able to repay the money within a month from the tailoring business he started. Later another 300 sols was loaned to a man who had been paying a moneylender 30 per cent per month on the money he borrowed to bury his father; after paying three times the amount of the loan, he still owed the entire amount of the principal. Now he would pay the credit union only one per cent per month. Even with so little to lend, the credit union was able to transform life for the family that bought the first bed they had ever possessed, or for the workman who was able to chop wood with the first axe he ever owned.

Loans in the San Juan Parish Credit Union since that

time in 1955 have made many things possible that were undreamed of before. There was a loan of 75,000 sols to explore a mine, another of 1,500 sols to buy a bull. A doctor bought Puno its first x-ray machine. A member borrowed 8,000 sols to invest in coffee, and then 30,000 a year later to develop his business. An Indian borrowed money to start a new local industry, making sandals out of old auto tires. All 20 of Puno's taxis were financed by the credit union. So were its four buses. Finally, the biggest loan of all, equal to nearly $7,000 in U.S. money, was granted to establish a laboratory in Puno which would manufacture animal serums and vaccines.

Dreaming even bigger dreams in 1958, Father McLellan drew his plans to move the people of Puno out of their dirt-floored mud hovels, into new homes with heat and running water. A 72-unit model housing development was built with co-operative labor, using mud bricks and other local materials, to show how it could be done. Down payments were made available to buyers at the credit union, which financed the whole project. More than 500 homes have already been built, and still more are on the way. One day soon, most of Puno's 40,000 Indians may well have moved out of their seventeenth century way of life, smack-dab into the twentieth century.

Look at the figures, to catch the breathless pace of the story. By the end of 1959, the San Juan Parish Credit Union had assets of 8,000,000 sols (about $350,000 in U.S. money). The credit union had granted 5,000 loans, for a total equivalent to a million U.S. dollars. Losses were far less than a tenth of one per cent, for who in Puno could endure the shame of failing his obligation to all his neighbors, whose money he borrowed through the credit union? Yet this period of dizzying growth included two years of serious drought, affecting every resident of the community. Worse yet, these were also years of inflation which cut the value of the Peruvian sol almost in half, from 16 to the dollar in 1955 to 28 to the dollar in 1959. Yet the credit union grew and grew, confounding every skeptical and unbelieving official in the capital at Lima.

Where did all the money come from? It came from the people themselves. The credit union had extracted capital where nobody knew or even suspected it existed. Some of it came from current income, money saved coin by coin, out of an income averaging $8 a month by United Nations estimates. Some of it came out of holes in the ground, where it had been hoarded in secret for a generation or more. And none of it—this is crucial—came from the banks or rich investors, because only the members can put money into a credit union. No, every solitary sol came from Puno's Indians themselves, showing the whole world that there is no limit to what people, no matter how poor, can achieve when they work together.

Father Dan sensed the universal longing behind the stolid, expressionless faces of the Quechua and Aymara Indians. He read the signs correctly. "If you want to know what human aspiration can mean," he told a "Yanqui" visitor, "you must see, as I have, a discarded light bulb hanging unexplained from a piece of string in the center of a dark and smoky hut built of mud. Here is a symbol of unspoken hope that some day, somehow, things will be better—and that (dare we believe it?) some day light might come into our dwelling." It was to such stirrings in his Indian people that Father Dan was able to respond, and to give substance to the hopes that lay behind their sullen and suspicious behavior toward all outsiders.

More than that happened, Father Dan points out. There have been more changes upward in Puno during the last five years than in the two centuries preceding. Yet there was no endless waiting for the government to act, no wishful waiting for factories to be built, nor for society to improve. The people saw that they were achieving these miracles themselves, now, and out of their own resources, without help from outside. It was done in ways that bolstered their pride in themselves and in their community, which they had preserved from their Inca ancestry through all the intervening years of humiliating and grinding poverty. With their credit union, they had brought these things to pass quickly, and in a way that was relatively easy. And by seeing how they could make all these wonderful things happen under their own control, they learned for the first time, first-hand, what democracy means and offers to mankind.

"If the credit union can work in Puno," Father Dan kept saying, "it can work any place else." His chance to prove it came when, with time off from his parish duties, he went to Lima. Here in the great city, in the shadow of the splendid office buildings and mansions pictured on the postcards, he found thousands living in the same kind of poverty he had seen in Puno. Here the people worked at city occupations and lived in city slums. They lived in rusty unlighted tin shacks instead of mud huts. But the poverty, the disease, the hostility, and the hopelessness were the same—or worse, because by lifting his eyes a man could see all about him the bitter contrasts of great wealth.

Yet soon the credit union began performing the same magic in Lima that had begun in Puno. Factory hands, waiters, cab drivers, and white-collar workers all began to benefit from the new credit unions that were established. Government officials, editors, and business executives became interested. Only the Communists did not like what they saw, because their promises were so rudely shoved aside by the rapid and tangible gains that appeared wherever a credit union was started.

Developments came quickly. Father Dan soon got welcome help from a field specialist working for the Credit Union National Association (CUNA), and later he traveled all the way to Madison, Wisconsin, for consultation and training. A Federation was set up in 1959, after 60 credit unions had been started, financed in part by donations from businessmen, bankers and credit unions in the U.S.A. and Canada who understood the importance of what was happening. On the invitation of the Peruvian Ministry of Public Health, Father McLellan journeyed from city to city along Peru's dry and dusty coastal plain, up and down the steep slopes of the towering Sierra, and even across the mountains into the steaming jungles of the Peruvian Amazon basin. He set up a training center in Lima at San Marcos University. He traveled outside Peru into Venezuela and Bolivia to help similar programs get started. By early 1961, Father Dan had 240 credit unions going in Peru alone.

In Callao, for example, Peru's most important port,

there is an interesting credit union serving more than 500 members of the Parish of San Rosa. Assets have already passed 500,000 sols, with most of the money out on purposeful loans to the members. Within the membership, the adults have also established another credit union for their children, to teach them the habits of thrift and working together for the common good. About 200 children belong. The funds are deposited in the adult credit union, but the children have their own board of directors, and their own credit committee to pass on the loan applications of the members. Already, these youngsters are learning to control their own money in ways wiser than their grandparents ever knew.

Credit unions are growing on the most unpromising soil. Far in the north of Venezuela may be found the Community of Tacuato Credit Union, which can be further located on the map in the area known as Paraguana, Falcon, Venezuela. The inhabitants of this arid and unlovely place swear that they have not seen rain in five years. Their wives daily sweep at least a pound of sand from their floors. Except for a lucky few who work for the oil refinery 30 miles away, the inhabitants live by raising goats, the only domestic animal which will stay alive in this place. Yet one year after a community credit union had been established for the 150 families living here, it had assets equal to $7,000 (U.S. dollars) and had made the community economically independent. Among other achievements, the credit union had financed the beginning of a new community industry, the production of salt from the salt flats nearby. Loans from the credit union had permitted the outright purchase of all needed machines and equipment.

On the outskirts of Valparaiso, Chile, is the Poblacion Graty Credit Union, serving the 200 employees of a textile mill. Not long ago, perhaps following the example of Puno, this credit union helped its members acquire a plot of land near the factory where they work and begin a housing project of their own. The first 15 homes were built completely on a self-help basis, with the members providing the labor themselves on free days and after regular working hours. At least 50 additional homes are planned.

In the industrial town of Chuquicamata, situated in the Chilean desert at an altitude of 9,000 feet, 13,000 miners have started a credit union of enormous potential. Enthusiasm runs high. A CUNA representative remembers that almost 2,000 members swarmed into the town stadium to hear a message from him, when he called on the credit union in 1959.

So it goes. Up till now, most of the credit unions in South America are located in Peru, with a sprinkling in Chile and a bare handful as yet operating elsewhere. But the results are already clear. In terms of real and living human needs, the coming of credit unions to South America is unquestionably one of the memorable economic stories of our times. The credit union crusade in South America is only beginning, but already it has put literally millions of dollars to work building new homes and new businesses, improving farms, schools, and medical facilities; and meanwhile removing the cruel burdens of poverty and lifelong debt and discouragement which have depressed this great continent since its written history began. Not only are its people raising themselves into economic salvation. Through their credit unions they are realizing that they have a contributing part in the present welfare and future development of their communities and their nations. They have learned confidence in the future. What began as a one-man assistance program in Puno has stirred the whole continent, and has emerged as the most formidable defense yet devised against the spread of Communism within its shores.

In the bountiful isles of the Caribbean, credit unions have long been a significant force. All told, there are nearly 500 credit unions serving these colorful and friendly spots and dots on the map, grouped into two leagues or federations centered in Jamaica and the West Indies, and in the Netherlands Antilles. They are providing their benefits to about 5,000,000 people, most of them with traditionally low incomes, but now caught up by the running tide toward economic freedom and political maturity which characterizes their region.

When the credit union was started in the parish of St. Thomas, on a sugar estate at Duckenfield—one of a hundred credit unions now operating in Jamaica—the island was then moving toward self-government, bringing many disturbing changes. The little community was troubled with political and trade union disputes, and there were many who were shaking their heads in dread of what might come. That was in the early '50's. Today they will tell you that it was the credit union which taught the people of the parish that they could disagree, democratic-style, and still work together, community-style. The credit union was the only organization that could bring within its membership the manager of the estate and his lowest-paid worker, the members of both political parties and the competing trade unions. Within five years the credit union had 400 members and $250,000 of assets. Multiply this experience of democracy in action by 500 credit unions, and you have the absorbing story of what is happening in the Caribbean.

Curacao and Aruba in the Netherlands Antilles had been traditionally poor islands until the big oil refineries came. Fifteen years after the refineries were built, what had happened? Now there were a few who lived in luxury, while many lived in poverty as hopeless as before. People who had never owned money did not know how to manage what they received. The relentless process that separates the rich from the poor went on until, after 14 months of tireless talking, a clergyman managed to start a credit union among a group which met, mainly to gamble their money away, at Colon, near Willemstad in Curacao. Three years later, there were 45 credit unions, with 10,000 members who had saved 350,000 guilders toward their own rising destiny.

Trinidad reports nearly 300 credit unions. Puerto Rico, listed statistically with the United States, has about the same number. Panama has 43, and British Honduras to the north has 42, with its own league organization. Only El Salvador among the Latin Republics of Central America has no credit unions.

Mexico, too, has about 300 credit unions, operating without the benefits of laws or a central organization, with only the support and inspiration of the church to sustain them. One noteworthy group is the Leo XIII Credit Union in Colonia Las Americas, a neighborhood on the outskirts of Mexico City. The average wage of the 4,000 people struggling for existence in this dingy area, one of the poorest in the capital city, is about $30 per month. But for the 100 who have joined the credit union, things are certainly looking up. Over a few years the credit union assets have gradually inched up to 150,-000 pesos, or about $12,000. The members have been everlastingly freed from the usurers and money lenders. As in Puno, there have been productive loans to buy taxicabs and to open small businesses, and there have been a great many providential loans to improve sub-standard homes. Most remarkable of all, the members have constructed a community center, which not only houses the credit union office, but also provides a medical clinic and an auditorium offering musical and recreational facilities! The members financed the entire undertaking through their funds in the credit union, making loans to members to purchase the building materials.

In the distant Philippines, once subject to the same Spanish flag as Latin America, there is another impressive example of a credit union movement meeting the fundamental economic needs of the population. The first credit union was started by the Rev. Allen Huber, who some time earlier had started the first Protestant church credit union in America, back in Indiana. Long delayed by government bureaucrats insisting that the group operate as a business corporation rather than a credit union, the first charter was finally granted in 1938 to the Church of Christ National Credit Union at Vigan, Ilocos Sur. After a Co-operative Administration Office was established in the Ministry of Commerce and Industry just before the outbreak of World War II, the movement grew to 30 credit unions by the time the first bombs fell on Clark Field.

Significantly, economists note that over 60 years the government tried no less than ten different systems to bring needed credit to the rural areas of the Philippines. Most of them failed. Credit unions, in fact, are the only self-help organizations which have been able to survive, and to grow, although separated by tremendous distances from the nearest source of assistance and instruction. Some of these determined credit unions continued operation throughout the war, changing monetary systems three times; those which were closed are, for the most part, back in operation. Today they number 500 or more. They are helping their members bury their dead, educate their children, buy homes, purchase rice lands, and obtain medical care. About 50,000 members, through their own efforts and not through government aid, have thus far met their own legitimate credit needs and have already written a significant chapter into the economic history of the Philippines. In 1960, a Credit Union League was organized with the aid of CUNA. In 1961 CUNA appointed a field man who will work in Manila, pointing to additional advances for the credit union movement at this decisive crossroads during the final half of the twentieth century.

Far to the south, across the sunny swells of the coral seas, another self-made miracle has come to pass in the Fiji Islands. There the native Fijians have almost overnight taken their place in the modern world and are heading off what appeared to be inevitable tragedy. The Fijians are said by travelers to be the most likable people on earth. But they have long been the despair of softhearted British administrators for persisting in their carefree ways while the Indians were proceeding to buy their island out from under them. The Indians had been imported to provide the sugar plantation labor the Fijians could not be persuaded to supply, trading their indentured time for citizenship status upon fulfilment of the contract. Bitterly ambitious—some say rapacious—the Indians have since overrun Fiji and have virtually taken over small business. One day very soon, it seemed, they would own the islands and would push the uncomplaining Fijians off into the sea. There was no visible alternative.

But changes came fast after gentle Father Ganey, a Jesuit priest who had much to do with the development of credit unions in British Honduras, was transferred to Suva at the request of administrators who knew of his work. With the encouragement of the government, and blessed with a sure and compassionate insight into the ways of his charges, Father Ganey traveled down the grassy paths from village to village, explaining the benefits the credit union could bring. He showed how the credit union would fit naturally into the framework of their village and tribal society, and how all its functions would be in keeping with the ceremony and ritual forms demanded by all matters of such gravity and importance. The credit union would provide tools for those who now scratched the earth with a stick to grow vegetables. It would provide nets for the fishermen. It would send the children to school. The villagers listened, and, one by one, after many months of patient work, there were 250 credit unions in Fiji, each in its own village. The credit union has adapted effortlessly to the council meetings, where the villagers sit in rows for formal deliberations, led by their elders. It is honored in village festivals, and at the kava-drinking ceremonials. It has enabled each village to provide for its own needs with hard cash money, and then to meet the insistent pressures of the commercial world. It happened almost overnight. It is almost unbelievable.

Nowhere is there a more dramatic example of what the credit union can do for people in underdeveloped countries. The credit union has flourished under the palm trees of Fiji in spite of low income, limited education, and all the handicaps inherent in a tribal society. Except, perhaps, for the native hair-do, Fiji is not unlike a thousand other localities where the credit union is the first financial institution which the average man can enter. In all these places until now, if there was any saving it was hoarding. Since a man could not take his few coppers to the bank, he buried them in the ground. When he had enough coins he might spend them for jewelry, or for gold teeth. Or he might invest in social prestige by means of a splendid party, or a fancy wedding for his child, or an elaborate funeral when a member of the family died. If he should need credit, there was only the money lender and a probable lifetime of debt. Indeed some debts were preserved on a traditional basis, with the lender's son inheriting the right to collect from the son of the borrower, from one generation to the next. The credit union has broken these vicious traditions, and has found the money to do so where nobody really believed it existed.

"In the beginning," said Roy Bergengren, "there was

usury." The credit union fights usury by accumulating savings, no matter how small, and by making loans at a reasonable rate. The handful of coppers is always welcome. The typical loan is the one the bank cannot accept—a few dollars for a fish net, or $10 for needles and thread to sell in the village, or still more for that most admired of man-made wonders, a sewing machine.

The system is magnificently simple. The credit union has demonstrably found in all peoples the ability to control, in a democratic way, their own financial instrument. You will find the ledger books in order, whether you visit a credit union in Peru or Fiji. By extension, the same principles of self-help become applied to the economic problems met by the members. Fishermen, for example, can collectively pay transportation costs of sending their catch to market for a fair price, rather than accept the arbitrary low price set by the trader who comes to the dock. In such ways the credit union trains leaders and businessmen and good citizens, who soon become aware that they are aiding the economy of their homelands while they help themselves.

These stories of underdeveloped countries do not minimize in the least the recent achievements of the credit union on such soil as Australia or New Zealand. Here the credit union, all over again, is meeting needs and providing positive benefits not dissimilar to those experienced by the related societies of the United States and Canada. But it is in the crucial and hungry underdeveloped areas of the world where the credit union may well have the most profound influence of our time—if it only gets there before it is too late.

All that is needed, credit union leaders say, is the money to speed up the job—money from some government, some international agency, some philanthropic foundation—to speed the credit union story around the world, as Edward Filene's money did for the United States a few years ago. So far, such missionary work has been spearheaded by CUNA and its World Extension Department, a mere handful of people with a mere handful of dollars set aside from the dues paid by individual credit unions. However willingly provided, more money is needed than this if the misison is half as urgent as they believe.

The credit union is no handout, they remind you, no packet of dollar bills tossed into the jungle or the desert to disappear after a brief moment of usefulness. The credit union is the finest tool of self-help we can offer today. It stands revealed and proven as the only quick and conclusive weapon against the age-old forces which tend to separate society ever more widely into millionaires and paupers. It is a complete and truthful answer to the cruel hoax of Communist promises. Those who have seen it work in Puno and Suva say the credit union can make a significant contribution to the world.

The expansive reach of credit unions now extends far beyond Fiji, into Samoa and Tonga and other realms of the South Pacific, and still farther, into Southeast Asia. There are credit unions now in Korea, and in Hong Kong, and in Malaya. Already credit unions are forming in the new and excited republics of Africa. Each frontier, however remote, adds strength and validity to the total cause. Each stresses the credit union in terms of the purpose and the pride and the progress so necessary to individual men of every condition and color. The living and potentially immortal root of every future free society is the creation and use of credit by everyday people, working and planning together for a peaceful world.

# Index